Dictionary of 1000
Jewish Proverbs

Dictionary of 1000 Jewish Proverbs

Edited by David C. Gross

HIPPOCRENE BOOKS
New York

For information, address:
HIPPOCRENE BOOKS, INC.
171 Madison Avenue
New York, NY 10016

Cataloging-in Publication Data
Dictionary of 1000 Jewish proverbs / edited by David C. Gross.
        p.   cm.
    ISBN 0-7818-0529-5
    1. Proverbs, Hebrew. 2. Proverbs, Hebrew—Translations into
English. 3. Proverbs, Jewish. I. Gross, David C., 1923-
PN6414.D53   1997
398.9'924—dc21   97-3556
                                     CIP

Printed in the United States of America.

Preface

Pick up a copy of the Hebrew Bible, and turn to one of its most popular books, the Book of Proverbs.

Think about it—thousands of years ago, the sages inscribed these pithy wise sayings so that all people, young and old, Jewish and non-Jewish, could read these axiomatic statements and—hopefully—learn from them.

Since that time, this ancient Jewish tradition has continued. Wherever Jews have lived during their long exile from their homeland, in virtually every corner of the globe, they have recorded more and more proverbs, to guide themselves and to instruct their offspring.

The proverbs, ancient and contemporary, encompassed a very wide range of subjects, reflecting lives that were often impoverished materially but rather rich spiritually. Through some osmotic process, these old and new proverbs became part of the Jewish people's heritage, and were not only passed on through the generations, but also expanded upon continually.

The wisdom, insight, and sharpness that come through are astounding, for it seems not much has changed in the past four thousand years.

Compiling this book was a very pleasurable assignment, as pages of the Bible, the Talmud, and so many other source books were consulted. There are now compilations of proverbs indigenous to Sephardi Jews, to Jews from Eastern Europe, and to Jews from North African and Asian lands, stretching across many centuries. The languages in which these proverbs first appeared were Hebrew, Yiddish, Aramaic and Ladino. By my own estimate there could already be in total some 6,000 to 7,000 Jewish proverbs.

The 1000 offered here are arranged by subject (on the left side of the page), followed by a transliteration into English from either

Hebrew or Yiddish, which is then followed by an English translation.

For easy reference, a complete index of the subjects appears at the back of the book.

The transliteration key is the same used in two other titles of mine published by Hippocrene Books, a Hebrew-English, and a Yiddish-English dictionary, both of which appear in Latin characters.

For simplicity's sake: the vowel a is sounded like the a in the word far; e is like the e in get; o is like the sound in for; u is like the oo in roof; ie is like the ee in feel, ei is like the y sound in the the word try and ai corresponds to the sound of a in the word face. Everything else is self-explanatory.

Are Jewish proverbs different from other proverbs? Yes and no. Yes, because in so many ways Jews are like other peoples, and their life experiences—and therefore their proverbs—reflect this very clearly. No, because they have through the ages undergone experiences that other nations have not, and this too is reflected in their proverbs.

One final note: the letter Y before a proverb indicates it is from Yiddish sources; A indicates Aramaic origin. All other proverbs stem from Hebrew sources.

Please enjoy this volume, and learn from it, just as I have learned a great deal in putting it together.

D.C.G.

A

Admission	1	Modeh al ha'emet chacham. A man who admits the truth is wise.
Advice	2	Shome'ah l'etzeem chacham. A wise man listens to advice
	3	Kal yoter liten aitza l'acher mee'l'atzmo. It's easier to advise others than oneself.
Affliction	4	Kol she'hakadosh baruch hu chafetz bo, m'dakk'o b'yisurim. Whom God favors, He tries with affliction.
Age	Y 5	Ah yunguer boim baigt zich, an alter boim vert tzubrochen. A young tree bends, an old tree breaks.
	6	B'chol gueel vagueel margeesh ha'adam b'ofen acher. At different ages, a person feels differently.
Agony	7	Ain adam nitpas bish'at tza'aro. A person should not be held responsible for what he said in agony.
Alone	Y 8	Afeelu in gan aiden, siz nit gut tzu zein alain. Even in heaven, it is not good to be alone.
	9	Lo tov heyot ha'adam l'vado. It is not good for man to be alone.

Ancestors	10	Eem ain adam oseh tov, al yivtach b'ma'asai avotav. If a man doesn't do good himself, he should not rely on his ancestors' deeds.
Angel	11	Ain malach echad oseh shtai shleechot. Not even an angel can fulfill two missions at once.
Anger	12	Ain m'ratzeem lo la'adam bish'at ca'aso. Don't try to placate a person when he is angry.
	13	Kol ha'ko'es kol meenai gaiheenom sholteem bo. All kinds of hellish devils rule an angry person.
	14	Af vachaimah—malachai chabala hem. Anger and fury—(these are) angels of destruction.
	15	Kumkumai galash al gueesai shafach. A boiling kettle spills hot water over its side.
Angry	16	Kol ha'ko'es, k'eelu oved avodah zarah. An angry person is like an idol worshiper.
Animal	17	A'sur l'adam sheyochal kodem sheyiten ma'achall liv'hemto. A man is not allowed to eat before he feeds his animal.
Answer	18	Ma'aneh rach, yasheev chaima. A gentle reply turns away rage.
	19	Heyai m'maher l'ha'azeen u'v'orech ru'ach hashave pitgam. Be quick to listen, and patiently repond wisely.
Anxiety	20	B'lo et, tazkeen had'agah. From anxiety a man grows prematurely old.
	21	Adam do'eg le'avar, niv'hal lhoveh, v'yareh le'ateed. A person worries about the past, is upset about the present, and fears the future.

Y 22   Besser tzen kleineh deiguis vee ain groiser.
Ten small worries are better then one giant one.

Arms   23   V'cheetetu charvotam l'eeteem
v'chaneetotaihem l'mazmairot.
And they shall beat their swords into
plowshares, and their spears into pruning
hooks.

Avarice   24   Ain dat eem ahavat betza.
There is no religion that favors avarice.

B

Bargain	25	Al ta'amod al hamekach b'sha'ah se'ain l'cha dameem. Don't bargain when you don't have any money.
Beauty	26	Sheker hachain v'hevel hayofee. Charm is deceitful, and beauty is vain.
	27	Shlosha marcheeveem da'ato shel adam: deera na'ah, eesha na'ah, v'kaileem na'eem. Three things please a man: a lovely home, a lovely wife, and lovely possessions.
Beginning	28	Kol hahatchalot kashot. All beginnings are difficult.
	29	Hitchalta? G'mor! When you start something, finish it!
Behavior	30	Tzareech adam latzet y'dai habree'ot, k'derech she'hu tzareech latzet y'dai hamakom. Behave before man as you would before God.
Believe	31	Hama'ameen, sh'ailot lo sha'al; habeeltee ma'ameen kol tshuva lo nishara mai'al. The believer does not question; the non-believer accepts no response.
Blind	32	Lifnai ivair lo titain mich'shol. Do not place an obstacle before a blind person.
	33	Tov ivair aineiyeem mai'ivair lev. Better blind of eye than blind of heart.

34 Mee ivair? She'aino rotzeh lirot or.
Who is blind? He who refuses to see the light.

Boasting 35 Al tit'halel b'yom machar kee lo taidah ma yeled yom.
Don't boast of tomorrow, for you know not what a day will bring.

36 Pree ha'ga'avah—seen'ah.
The fruit of boasting (or pride) is—hatred.

Body 37 Eiyeen ro'ah, v'ha'lev chomed, v'hagoof oseh et ha'avairot.
The eye sees, the heart desires, and the body sins.

38 Eer k'tanah, zeh hagoof.
The body is a small city by itself.

Books 39 Seem s'fareem chavairecha.
Make friends of your books.

40 Hasefer v'hasayif yardu m'choracheem min hashameiyeem.
The book and the sword descended from heaven together.

41 Mi'yad hasefer hayedi'ah nitna, meepee hachayeem hahavanah.
Books provide knowledge, life furnishes understanding.

42 Marbeh s'fareem, marbeh chochma.
The more books, the more wisdom.

Boredom 43 Habatala m'vee'ah leedai shee'a'mum.
Laziness brings on boredom.

Born 44 Et laledet, v'et lamoot.
There is a time to be born, and a time to die.

Borrower 45 Eved loveh l'eesh malveh.
A borrower becomes enslaved to the lender.

46 Der vos vil borguen, zal er kumen morguen. *Y*
He who wishes to borrow—can come tomorrow.

Bread 47 Lo al halechem l'vado yichyeh ha'adam.
A person does not live by bread alone.

48 Al pat lechem yifsha gaver.
A man will sin for a piece of bread.

49 Shlach lach'm'cha al pnai hamayeem kee b'rov yameem timtsa'enah.
Cast your bread upon the waters; after many days, you will find it.

Brevity 50 L'olam yihiyu d'varav shel adam m'utin lifnai hakadosh baruch hu.
The words of a man to God should be brief.

Bribe 51 B'heekanes hashochad derech hapetach, yivrach hayosher derech hachalon.
When a bribe enters through the front door, honesty departs through the window.

Bride 52 Ain kalah m'cho'eret b'yom chatunatah.
There is no ugly bride on her wedding day.

Bridegroom 53 Chatan domeh l'melech.
A bridegroom is like a king.

Broom 54 Birtzot haboreh, hamatatai yoreh.
If the Creator wills it, the broom can shoot a bullet.

Brother 55 Acheecha hagadol c'aveecha.
Your older brother should be honored as your father.

56 Tov shachen karov me'ach rachok.
Better a neighbor nearby than a distant brother.

Bygones *A* 57 Ma she'haya, haya; mai d'hava, hava.
What was, was; what is, is (Let bygones, be bygones).

C

Cake	58	Hamechapes oogah, m'abed et halechem. Whoever seeks cake, loses his bread.
Calling	59	Ain l'cha adam ohev bven-umanuto aval hechacham ohev ben-umanuto. With the exception of scholars, men don't like others in the same vocation.
Candle	59	Ner l'echad, ner l'me'ah. One person's candle furnishes light for many.
Carpenter	61	Kol nagar she'ain b'yado argalya shelo—aino nagar. Every carpenter without his tools—is no carpenter.
Cash	62	Kol she'hakesef b'yado, yado al ha'elyon. So long as you have some cash, you're on top.
Caution	63	Hanizhar yaguee'ah l'cheftzo. The cautious person will reach his goal.
	64	Maichukai hazeheerut hu livlee lihizaher yoter midei. A basic rule of caution: Don't be overly cautious.
Censure	65	Matcheeel bignut u'misayem b'shevach. Start with censure, and wind up with praise.

Certainty	66	Ain vadei she'ain bo safek. There's no certainty that doesn't include some doubt.
Chance	67	Kee et vafegah yikreh et kulam. Time and chance happen to everyone.
Change	68	Kol ham'shanah yado al hatachtonah. When you change an agreement, you are the loser.
	69	M'shaneh makom, m'shaneh mazal. When you change your place (residence) you change your luck (for the better).
	70	Kol shinu'ee, shanu'ee. Every change is uncertain.
Character	71	Bishlosha d'vareem ha'adam nikar: koso, keeso, ka'aso. Three things show a man's character: his drinking, his pocket, and his anger.
	72	L'olam y'hai adam rach ka'kaneh, v'al y'hai kashe ka'erez. A man should always be pliable like a reed, not rigid like a cedar.
	73	Al ta'aroch adam al pee madotav elah al pee mee-dotav. Don't judge a person by his clothes, but by his characteristics.
Charity	74	Gadol ha'oseh tzedaka baseter yoter mimoshe rabbenu. He who gives charity anonymously is greater than Moses.
	75	Lo tikpotz et yadcha me'acheecha ha'evyon. Don't shut your hand from your needy brother.
	76	Tzedaka tatzeel mimavet. Charity will save you from death.

77   Shkula tzedaka k'negued kol hamitzvot.
     Giving charity outweighs all the religious com-
     mandments.

78   Afeelu anee hamitparnes min hatzedaka ya'aseh
     tzedakah.
     Even a poor recipient of charity should give char-
     ity.

79   Chaveeva g'meelut chasadeem min tzedaka.
     Kindliness is more important than giving charity.

80   Tzedaka ma'arechet yamav u'shnotav shel adam.
     Giving charity enlarges a person's days and years.

Charm   Y 81   Chain iz besser fun shainkeit.
               Charm is better than beauty.

Cheap   Y 82   In gueneem, an ochs hot dervert a groshen,
               ober afeelu a groshen ken m'nit guefinin.
               In hell, an ox is worth a penny, but even a
               penny is not to be found.

Childhood 83   Hayaldut v'hashacharut—hevel.
               Childhood and youth—are vanity.

               84   Beemai hayaldut davar lomdeem, l'et zikna al
               ameeto omdeem.
               What you learn in childhood is proven true in
               old age.

Children   85   Eem lo t'chabed horecha, lo y'chabducha
               banecha.
               If you do not honor your parents, your
               children will not honor you.

               Y 86   Av echad yachol l'farnes asara baneem, v'asara
               baneem ainam ycholeem l'farnes av echad.
               One father can support ten children, but ten
               children can't support one father.

Y 87 Dee kinder veren groiser un dee elteren veren alter.
The children are growing up, and the parents are getting older.

88 Hak'taneen, c'ev rosh; hag'doleem, c'ev lev.
Small children, a headache; big children, heart-ache.

89 Ain gueshem blee ra'ameem, v'ain laida blee chavaleem.
There's no rain without thunder, and no children born without pain.

Choice 90 Kol hamarbeh livchor, al yirgaz al asher alah b'chelko.
If someone chooses too much, he shouldn't get angry at his final lot.

City 91 Kol eer she'ain ba yerek, ain talmeed chacham rasha'ee ladur ba.
A scholar may not live in a city that has no plant life or verdure.

Clean *A* 92 Lu nika eesh'eesh lifnai pitcho, v'nuku eretz v'chutzot.
If everyone cleaned his own doorstep, all the streets would be clean.

Y 93 Der teirster zaiguer ken nit veizen mer vee zechtzig minit in yeden shtundeh.
The costliest clock can only show sixty minutes in every hour.

Clothes 94 Echol l'fee da'atcha, u'l'vash l'fee haskamat achaireem.
Eat what you want, but dress in fashion.

95 Bigdai adam m'ramzeem al meedotav.
A man's clothes hint at his inner character.

Community 96 Al tifrosh min hatzibur.
Don't detach yourself from the community.

Controversy 109 Dor holech v'dor ba v'hamachloket l'olam omedet.
Generations come and go, but controversy lasts forever.

110 S'tam akshan, am ha'aretz.
Whoever argues for the sake of argument is a boor.

Conversation 111 L'chol moshav—d'vareem.
When people meet, they should speak.

112 Miseechato shel adam nikar mee hu.
A person is recognized by his conversation.

Counsel 113 Marbeh aitza, marbeh t'vunah.
The more counsel, the more understanding.

Courage Y 114 Farloirene guelt nit gueferlech. Farloirene mut, als iz farloiren.
It's not so terrible when you lose money. When courage is lost, all is lost.

Crime 115 Hachet atzmo, hu ha'onesh.
The crime itself is the punishment for crime.

Crown 116 Shlosha k'tareem hem: Torah, k'huna, v'malchut. Keter shem tov oleh al kulam.
There are three crowns: Bible, priesthood, royalty. But the crown of a good name surpasses them all.

Curse 117 Sof kill'lat chinam lashuv el hamekalel.
A curse without reason will in the end return to the curser.

Custom 118 Haminhag m'vatel et hahalachah.
Custom cancels out the law.

119 Hakol k'minhag hamedinah.
Everything follows the custom of the country.

D

Danger   120   L'olam al ya'amod adam bimkom sakana
she'oseem lo nes.
A person should avoid a dangerous place,
expecting a miracle to rescue him.

Darkness   121   Tzazreech l'hagbeer et ha'or tachat l'hilachem
bachoshech.
We should bolster the light rather than fight
the darkness.

Daughter   122   Ain habat maguedet elah l'eema.
A daughter confides only in her mother.

123   Bat l'hasa'ah—oneeya l'hatana.
Marrying off a daughter is like loading cargo on
a ship.

124   Mishehee'see'a ain l'aveeha r'shut ba.
When a daughter marries, her father's jurisdic-
tion over her ends.

Daughter-   125   Harotzeh l'hochee'ach et bito, mochee'ach et
in-Law   calato.
Whoever wants to chastise his daughter,
rebukes his daughter-in-law.

Dead   126   B'chu la'availeem v'lo la'aveda, shehu limnucha,
v'anu l'anacha.
Weep for the mourners, not for the dead; they
have gone to their rest, and we are left to
lament.

	127	Mitzvah l'kayem divrai ha'met. It is a sacred command to fulfill the wishes of a dying person.
Death	128	Ain adam m'shateh bish'at meeta. Nobody at death's door acts mockingly.
	129	Yoter tov hameeta me'hakalon. Death is preferable to dishonor.
	Y 130	Besser a gringuer toit vee a shveren lebn. An easy death is better than a hard life.
Debt	131	Ain d'aga c'da'agat hachov. There's nothing more worrisome than a debt.
Deed	132	Emor m'at v'aseh harbeh. Say little and do much.
Divorce	133	Lo yisa eesha v'da'ato l'gorsha. A man should not marry and plan to divorce his wife.
Do	134	Hana'aseh ain l'hasheev. What is done cannot be undone.
Doctor	*Y* 135	A mentsh ken shtarben afeelu ohn a dokter. A person can die even without a doctor.
	136	A'sur ladur b'eer she'ain ba rofeh. It is forbidden to live in a city without a physician.
Dog	137	Ha'ochel bashook domeh l'chelev. He who eats in the market place is like a dog.
Doubt	138	Hasefekot a'su et ha'anasheem chachameem. Doubts have made people wise.
	139	Birvot hada'at, yigdal hasafek. As knowledge grows, so do the doubts.
Dowry	*Y* 140	A nad'n un a yerusha hob'n nit a simen fun brocha. A dowry and an inheritance do not portend a blessing.

Dream   141   Ain mar'een lo l'adammehirhurai libo.
                  In his dream, a person sees only wishful
                  thinking.

            142   Divrai chalomot lo ma'aleen v'lo moreedeen.
                  Dreams do not add to or subtract from under-
                  standing.

Drink   143   Hashoteh koso b'vat achat harai zeh gargran.
                  Whoever drinks his glass in one gulp is seen as
                  greedy.

Drop   144   Avaneem shachaku mayeem.
                  Constant dripping eats away at a stone.

Drunk   145   Shikor shemitpalel k'eelu oved avoda zara.
                  A drunkard at prayer is regarded as an idol
                  worshiper.

Duty   146   Yesh chova musareet achat, shedavka
                  hamusaraneem m'zalz'leem ba, ad k'dai avon
                  pleelee—hachova lehanot me'olamo shel
                  hakadosh baruch hu.
                  There is one moral duty that moralists
                  underrate almost criminally—the duty to enjoy
                  God's world.

E

Ear	147	Oznayeem lakotel. Walls have ears.
	148	Yizm'oo oznecha ma shepeecha omer. Let your ears hear what your mouth says.
Eating	149	Achol v'shato kee machar namoot. Eat and drink for tomorrow we die.
	A 150	Ad arba'een shnain maichla m'alai, mikan v'ailach mishtai m'alai. Till age forty, it is better to eat. After that, drinking is better.
	151	Achal v'lo halach arba amot, acheelato markevet. If you don't walk (four cubits) after eating (and before bed), your food remains undigested.
	152	Ichlu k'dai shetichyu. Eat so that you may live.
Enemy	153	Aizehu guibor? Ha'oseh son'o l'ohavo. Who's a hero? He who turns his enemy into his friend.
Envy	154	Tov she'y'kanu b'cha mai'asher yanudu l'cha. It's better to be envied than pitied.
Equal	*Y* 155	In bod alle zeinen gleich. *Y* Everyone is equal in the bath house.

156   Shivyon b'nai adam hee mila raika kol od ain
shivyon l'amai olam.
The equality of man is an empty phrase so long as it
does not exist among the world's peoples.

Evil   157   Ain ra she'ain bo tov.
There is no evil without some good.

158   Yetzer ha'ra rosho matok v'sofo mar.
At first the evil inclination is sweet; at the end
it's bitter.

159   Al y'dai yetzer ha'ra hashaneem mitkatzrot.
A person's years are shortened by evil desire.

Experience   160   Ain chacham k'va'al hanisayon.
No one is wiser than the man of experience.

Y 161   A mentsh ken lernen zibitzig yor un tzum sof
shtarben a nar.
A person can study for seventy years, and at
the end die a fool.

Eye   162   Lo tishba ayeen lirot, v'lo timaleh ozen
mishmo'a.
The eye is not satisfied with seeing, nor the ear
with hearing.

F

Face	163	B'fanav yivada maskeel. A man's intelligence is reflected in his face.
Faith	164	Ha'emunah hee l'ma'ala mehada'at v'hahasaga. Faith is over and above knowledge and understanding.
	165	Emunah hee yesod v'shoresh kol hakedusha. Faith is the foundation and root of all sanctity.
	166	Ha'emunah aina ma'arechet shel mishpateem elah derech shel chayeem. Faith is not a whole series of axioms but a whole way of life.
Family	167	Blee chayai mishpacha lo yibaneh am. Without family life, no nation can be built.
	168	Hapogaim et atzmo pogaim mishpachto eemo. Whoever discredits himself, discredits his family too.
Fate	Y 169	Oib a mentsh iz bashert tzu dertrinken veren, vet er farleeren zein leben afeelu in a lefele vasser. If a person is fated to drown, he'll lose his life even in a teaspoon of water.
	170	Chacham she'aino muchshar l'hashleem im goralo, aino b'cheenat chacham. A wise man who is unable to accept his fate is not really wise.

Father 171 Avot achlu voser v'sheenai baneem tikhena.
Fathers ate sour grapes, and their sons' teeth
were set on edge.

172 Ma'asai avot seeman l'vaneem.
A father's good deeds are a good example for his
sons.

173 Shimu baneem musar av, v'haksheevu l'da'at
beena. Kee lekach tov natatee lachem, toratee al
ta'zovu.
Sons, heed a father's teaching. Listen and learn
discernment. For I give you good instruction, do
not forsake my teaching.

Fault 174 Ohavee yoranee yitronee, v'oyevee yodee'ainee
chesronee.
My friend tells me of my virtue, my enemy
notes my fault.

Favor 175 G'dola g'milut chasadeem yoter min tzedaka.
A favor granted is greater than charity.

176 Eem ta'aseh chesed la'adam tihiye g'veero; v'eem
t'kabel chesed, tihiye aseero; v'eem lo titztarech,
tihiye chavero.
If you do a person a favor, you'll be his superior;
if he does one for you, his inferior; and if neither, you'll be his friend.

177 Eem ta'aseh l'eesh tovah, al tireh lo chovah.
If you do someone a kindness, don't see it as a
debt he must repay.

Fear 178 Al tira mipachad pitom.
Do not be afraid of sudden fear.

179 Hayarai min he'aleem al yelech laya'ar.
If you're fearful of the leaves, don't enter the for-
est.

Flattery	180	Miyom shegavar egrofa shel chanupa, nitavtu hadeeneem. When flattery clenched its fist, the laws were corrupted.
	Y 181	Kainer vet gueshtrofen vern far unterchanfenun zich. Nobody gets punished for flattering someone.
Flesh	182	Marbeh basar, marbeh rimah. The more flesh, the more worms.
Flour	183	Eem ain kemach, ain torah. If there's no flour, there's no study of the Bible.
Folly	184	Eevelet simcha l'chasar lev. Folly is a joy only to a person lacking in understanding.
	185	Yakar michochma, mikavod sichlut m'at. A small drop of folly outweighs much wisdom and honor.
	186	Kol amal ha'adam, l'fee hu. All of man's work is to feed his mouth.
Fool	187	K'seeleem yisn'u da'at. Fools hate knowledge.
	188	Peti ya'ameen l'chol davar. A simpleton believes anything.
	189	Gam eveel machareesh, chacham yechashev. Even if a fool remains silent, he is considered wise.
	190	Ra'oo'ee lechacham sheya'aseh atzmo peti bimko-mot. Sometimes it's worthwhile for a wise man to play the role of a fool.
	Y 191	Besser mit a nar tzu farleeren aider mit a klugen tzu guevinen. It's better to lose to a fool than to win from a smart guy.

Forgetting	192	Tovat yom tishkach hara'ah, v'ra'at yom tishkach tovah. One day's happiness and you forget the bad; one bad day and you forget the good.
Forgiveness	193	Hamevakesh matu mechaver lo mevakesh yoter mishalosh p'ameem. If you ask forgiveness from a friend, shouldn't ask more than three times.
Friend	194	Eesh re'eem l'hitro'aiah. A man with friends must show he is friendly.
	195	Ohev emunah, ohev t'kof u'motz'o matza hon. A loyal friend is a strong defense; such a friend is a treasure.
	196	Al titosh ohev yashan kee chadash lo yidomeh lo. Yayeen chadash ohev chadash, v'yashan achar tishtenu. Do not abandon an old friend, for a new one does not compare. A new friend is like new wine—you will drink it with pleasure.
	197	Ohev chadash mipnai chadash al totzee. Don't throw out an old friend for a new one.
	198	Ain michman cachaverim. There is no treasure like friends.
Fruit	199	Kol ilan tov nosai pree tov. Every good tree bears good fruit.
Future	200	Al tetzar tzarat machar. Don't worry about the future.

G

Gambling	201	Hakubi'yustus over al kol aseret hadibrot. The gambler breaks all of the Ten Commandments.
Generation	202	Dor holech, v'dor ba, v'ha'aretz l'olam omedet. A generation comes and a generation goes, and the earth abides forever.
	203	Dor dor v'dorshav, dor dor v'chachamav. Every generation has its advocates, and every generation has its sages.
	204	Hanadeev hashalem hu asher noten tadeer m'at o rav kodem she'yishalu mimenu. A genuinely generous person always gives (charity), a little or much, before he is asked.
Gift	205	Son'ai matanot yichyeh. A person who hates gifts will live.
	206	Matana al m'nat l'hachazeer. To receive a gift means you have to return a gift.
	207	Hamekabel et chavero b'sever paneem yafot, k'eelu natan lo kol matanot tovot sheba'olam. Whoever welcomes his friend with a smile, it's as though he gave his friend the finest gifts in the world.
Glutton	208	Kol sovai v'zolel yivaresh. Every glutton and drunkard will be impoverished.

Good	209	L'ma'an telech b'derech toveem, v'orchot tzadeekeem tishmor. Follow the way of the good; keep to the paths of the righteous.
	210	Al timna tov mib'alav bihiyot yadcha la'asot. Don't withhold the good where it is due, if it's in your power to do it.
	211	Ain tov she'ain ba ra. There is no good without some bad in it.
Good deed	212	Gadol hama'aseh min ha'oseh. Whoever influences another to do a good deed is greater than the doer.
	213	M'galg'leen z'chut al y'dai zakai. Good deeds are performed by good people.
	214	Eem aseeta mitzva al t'vakesh matan s'chara mi-yad l'yad. If you did a good deed, don't ask for an immediate reward.
Gossip	215	B'efes etzeem tichbeh esh, u'v'ain guirgan yishtok madon. Fire dies for lack of wood; if there's no whispering, gossip stops.
	216	Kee tishma davar ra, v'histarto sheva amot ba'adama. If you hear an evil thing, bury it seven cubits deep.
Grace	217	Chen eesha al ba'ala. A wife gives grace to her husband.
	218	Chen hamakom al yoshvav. A place of grace gives grace to those who reside there.
Great	219	Eem lo tish'af ligdolot, ad hak'tanot lo tavo. If you don't aspire to great things, you won't attain small things.

Greatness	220	Kol hamechazer al hag'dula, g'dula borachat mimenu; kol haborai'ach min hag'dula, hag'dula m'chazeret acharav. Whoever pursues fame and greatness, they flee from him; whoever shuns greatness, it comes after him.
Greed	221	Ain nimas me'ohev betza kee gam et nafsho yimkor. Nobody is more contemptible than a greedy man; he would even sell his soul.
Greeting	222	Hevai makdeem bishlom kol adam. Be first in greeting every person.
Grief	*A* 223	Gavrai gueebareen katla d'vaya. Even a hero is destroyed by grief.
Guest	224	Yom aleph, ore'ach; yom bet, tore'ach; yom gimmel, sore'ach. First day, a guest; second day, a pest; third day, a nuisance.
	225	Ore'ach tov omer: Baruch ba'al habayit. A good guest proclaims: Blessed is the host.
	226	Ore'ach machnees ore'ach—harai zeh m'guneh. When one guest brings an uninvited guest, that is improper.
	227	Ore'ach she'ba b'yadayeem raikot aino zocheh l'varuch haba. A guest who comes empty-handed does not deserve a warm welcome.

H

Habit	228	Ee efshar l'fee teva ha'adam sh'yanee'ach kol ma shehirgueel bo pitom. It's impossible for a person to give up everything he has become habituated to.
	229	Hamidot hatovot niknot b'herguel. Virtues result from good habits.
	230	Herguel na'aseh teva. Habits eventually become second nature.
Half	231	Chatzee shoteh garu'a mishoteh gamur. Half a fool is worse than a complete fool.
	232	Yish'renu ha'el mechatzee chacham umechatzee rofeh. May the Lord guard us from a half-fool and a half-physician.
Hand	233	Al t'hee p'tucha yadcha lakachat, u'kfutza b'toch matan. Your hand should not be wide open to take, and clenched shut when you return.
	234	Hamagbeesh yado al chavero af al pee shelo hi-kahu nikra rasha. Raising your hand against a friend, even if you don't hit him, is evil.
	235	Rabot hayadayeem m'shabrot chomotayeem. Many hands can shatter stout walls.

Handwriting 236   K'tav ha'adam moreh al sichlo.
One's handwriting delineates his intelligence.

Happening   237   Ma shelo yikreh b'elef shaneem alul likrot
b'achat hadakot.
What did not happen in one thousand years
could happen in the next moment.

Happiness   238   Lo kol mee shesame'ach hayom same'ach
l'machar.
Not everyone who is happy today will be
happy tomorrow.

239   Kol mee sh'aino same'ach b'chelko nikra rash.
A person who is not happy in his lot is called a
wretch.

240   Haderech hatova b'yoter l'hasagat ha'osher hee
shelo l'chapes oto.
The best way to find happiness is not to search
for it.

241   Torah g'dola hee lihiyot m'ushar.
It's not easy to know how to achieve ahppiness.

Harm   Y 242   Tzen soneem kenen nit tu'en die shod'n vos a
mentsh ken tu'en tzu zich.
Ten enemies cannot do the harm to someone
that he can do to himself.

Haste   243   P'ree hamehirut—charata.
The result of haste is—remorse.

Hate   244   Shkula sinat chinam k'negued shalosh averot:
avodah zara, gueelu'ee arayot, u'shefichat
dameem.
Causeless hate is equal to three sins: idolatry,
incest and bloodshed.

245   B'nai adam soneem l'davar sh'ainam m'veeneem.
People hate what they do not understand.

246   Sinat chinam hee cholee kasha.
Baseless hate is a serious disease.

| Haughty | 247 | B'chol ha'averot kulan muchrach adam la'asot aizeh ma'aseh. Ulam ba'averah shel ga'avah shochev lo prakdan al mitato m'fahek v'omer b'libo: gadol anee! |

With every other sin a person must do something. With haughtiness, one lies on his bed, yawns, and says to oneself: I'm great.

Health 248 Ain osher ka'bree'ut.
There is no wealth—like health.

249 Adam baree ohev et hachayeem mitivo.
A healthy person instinctively loves life.

Heart 250 Yetzer lev ha'adam ra min'urav.
Man's heart (inclination) is bad from his youth.

251 Gam bis'chok yichav lev.
Even in laughter, the heart hurts.

252 Lev same'ach yaiteev paneem.
A merry heart makes for a cheerful countenance.

253 Ain adam yodai'ah ma sheb'libo shel chavero.
Nobody knows what's in his friend's heart.

Hero 254 Aizehu guibor? Hakovesh et yitzro.
Who is a hero? One who conquers his lust.

History 255 Galgal hu sh'chozer ba'olam.
A wheel always comes around to the starting point.

Hole 256 Chor katan yatbee'ah oniyah g'dola.
A small hole can sink a big ship.

Holiness 257 Mee shelo ta'am ta'am chet lo huchshar likdusha.
Whoever has not tasted sinfulness does not qualify for holiness.

Home 258 Baito—zo ishto.
His home is—his wife.

259   Kol bayit she aino asu'ee limot hachom v'limot
hag'shameem aino bayit.
Any home not built for hot days or for rains is
not a home.

260   Simcha l'adam b'sha'ah shehu dar b'toch shelo.
A man is happy when he lives beneath his own
roof and tree.

Honor   261   Aizehu m'chubad? Hamechabed et habree'ot.
Who is honored? He who honors his fellow
men.

262   Lifnai kavod, anava.
Before honor comes humility.

263   Kabdaihu v'chashdaihu.
Honor him but also be wary of him.

264   Hakavod hu yoter m'uleh min ha'osher, she'ain
ha'osher kee eem klee l'haguee'a el hakavod.
Honor is greater than wealth; wealth is only an
instrument to attain honor.

Hope   *A* 265   Tochelet m'mushacha machala lev.
Hope deferred makes the heart sick.

266   Kol z'man she'adam chai yesh lo tikva; met
v'avda tikvato.
So long as a person is alive, he has hope; when
he's dead, his hope is gone.

267   Ha'eesh asher chadal mikavot chadal meheyot.
The man who stopped hoping, stopped living.

Hospitality   268   G'dola hachnasat orcheen yoter mehash'camat
beit hakneset.
Being hospitable is more important than
attending synagogue service early in the
morning.

House   269   Bayit sheyesh bo mackloket—sofo lecharov.
A house divided against itself—its future is to
be destroyed.

Humility	270	Anaveem yirshu eretz. The humble will inherit the earth.
	271	Gadol ha'erez l'fee tzilo, v'gadol eesh l'fee anvato. A cedar's size is measured by its shade, and a man by his humility.
Humor	272	G'dola midat hahumor sheprusha gam havanat atzmo u'vikoret atzmo...kol makom she'ata motzeh he'der humor, ata motzeh katnut hamocheen. Humor is an important asset: it means understanding and self-criticism. Where humor is absen, you'll find small-mindedness.
Hunchback Y	273	Der hoiker ken nit zai'en zein hoik.Y The hunchback cannot see his own hump.
Hunger	274	Aitza u'dvar s'fatayeem lo yasbee'u nefesh r'aiva. Advice and empty words will not satisfy an empty stomach.
Husband	275	Kalon laguever heyot eshet ishto. It's a disgrace for a man to be his wife's wife.
	276	Haba'al sorer b'vaito eem ha'eesha aina babayit. When the wife is away, the husband is master of the house.

I

Immortality 286

Almavet hu b'vadei reguesh na'eem m'od, b'yichud kol od ha'eeesh chei.

Immortality is surely a pleasant feeling, especially when the individual is still alive.

Impossible 287

Teven lo nitan l'avad l'avdecha, u'levaineem omreen lanu asu.

It's impossible to fashion bricks without straw.

288

Ha'efshar lishnai m'lacheem she'yishtamshu b'keter echad?

Can two kings wear one crown?

289

Hacheresh shama mipee ha'ilem kee ha'eever ra'ah et hachiguer ratz.

The deaf person heard from his mute friend that the blind man saw the lame man running.

Indecisive 290

Pose'ach al shtai has'ipim.

He hesitates on two threshholds.

Independence 291

Harbeh yoter kashesh lichyot chayai chofesh, yesh l'rochsha.

It's harder to live a life of independence; it must be earned.

Indifference 292

Ain klai-zeiyin chazak min ha'adishut; lo t'natzchuha.

There is no stronger weapon than indifference; you won't beat it.

Influence 293

Hashpa'ah shelo mida'at erka yoter gadol.

Unobtrusive influence has the most value.

Ingratitude 294

Ten l'adam egozeem v'hu yizrok et haklipot al panecha.

Give a person peanuts, and he'll throw the shells in your face.

Inheritance Y 295

Az a mentsh kumt optzunemen die yerusha, darf er amol oich batzolen far die l'veiyeh.

When someone claims an inheritance, he sometimes has to pay for the funeral.

Insatiable	296	Eesha v'eretz v'kares lo yed'u sava. A woman, land, and a belly are insatiable.
Insult	297	Adam gadol aino no'ach l'he'alev. A great person does not easily become insulted.
Intelligence	298	N'von davar: shemaiveen davar mitoch davar. An intelligent person is one who understands one thing extracted from another.
Intention	299	Tzreecheem ladun et ha'adam al pee shenitkaven la'asot v'lo al pee ma she'asah. A person must be judged by what he intended to do, not what he did.
	300	Tov m'at b'chavana, meharbeh blee cavanah. A little together with intention is better than a lot without.
Interest	301	Mee shemalveh b'ribeet aino yarai min hakadosh baruch hu. Whoever lends (money) with interest is not God-fearing.
Interpretation	302	Lev enosh yagueed shi'eeyotav mishiva tzofeem al mitzpeh. A man's heart tells him of his opportunities better than seven watchmen on the lookout tower.
	303	Shiveem paneem latorah. There are seventy ways of interpreting the Bible.
Investment	304	Lo y'hai adam noten kol mamono b'zaveet achat. Don't put all your money into one corner.
Iron	305	Habarzel maguen aval gam ha'met yameet. Iron protects, but it can also kill.

Israel   306   Ha'umot ba'ot l'hitgarot im hakadosh baruch
                      hu, v'ain yecholeen. Ma oseem? Mitgareem b'yis-
                      rael.
                      The nations of the world wish to irritate the
                      Lord, but they can't. What do they do? They vex
                      Israel instead.

J

Jealousy	307	R'kav atzamot—kina. Jealousy rots the bones.
	308	Kina v'af yikatzru yameem. Jealousy and anger will shorten one's days.
	309	Me'ah mitot v'lo kina achat. Jealousy is far, far worse than death.
	A 310	Kol man d'rachem v'la kasher ima kina, lav r'cheemutai r'cheemutah. Whoever loves without any jealousy, his love is no love.
	311	Kina—barzel shineha. Jealousy has teeth made of iron.
Jerusalem	312	Asara kabeen yofee yardu la'olam, tisha natla yerushalayeem v'echad kol ha'olam kulo. Ten measures of beauty descended on the world; nine went to Jerusalem, and one to the rest of the world.
Jewelry	313	Ain tachsheet na'eh elah im hagoof m'udan. If the wearer is elegant, so is the jewelry.
	314	Mayeem shachaku even—va'adayeem lev eesha. Water wears away stones—and jewelry the heart of a woman.
Jews	315	Kol yisrael araivin zeh bazeh. All Jews are responsible, one for another.

Y 316   Siz shver tzu zein a yid.
It's hard to be a Jew.

Joy   317   Ra'eetee kee ain tov me'asher yismach ha'adam b'ma'asav.
There's nothing better than that a person should enjoy his work.

318   Lech echol b'simcha lach'm'cha, u'shtai b'lev tov yainecha.
Eat your bread joyously, drink your wine with a merry heart.

319   Mee she'chei b'simcha oseh r'tzon kono.
Whoever enjoys his life is doing the Creator's will.

Judaism   320   Ain bayahadut af shemetz shel pesemiyut, u'shleelat hachayeem zara caleel l'rucha.
There is no hint of pessimism in Judaism; negation of life is totally alien to its spirit.

Judge   321   Hevai dan kol adam l'cahf z'chut.
Judge every person with the benefit of the doubt.

Justice   322   Tzedek, tsedek tirdof.
Justice and only justice shall you pursue.

323   Al shlosha d'vareem ha'olam kayam: al ha'deen, al ha'emet, v'al hashalom.
The world is sustained by three things: justice, truth and peace.

324   Yikove hadeen et hehar!
Let the law cut through the mountain!

325   Mutav she'teepaga me'ee tzedek me'asher ta'aseh avel l'zulatcha.
It's betther that you suffer an injustice than you commit one.

K

Kill	326	Haba l'horguecha, hashkem l'horgo. If someone comes to kill you, rise early and kill him first.
Kindness	327	Chesed v'emet al ya'azvucha. May kindness and truth not forsake you.
	328	Al pee shlosha d'vareem ha'olam omed: torah, avodah, g'milut chasadeem. The world rests on three things: the Bible, religious worship, and deeds of loving kindness.
	329	Bishvil hachesed ha'olam mitkayem. The world exists for the sake of kindness.
King	330	Afeelu adam katzar v'hu mitmaneh l'melech, na'aseh aroch. When a short man is made king, he seems to grow tall.
Kiss	331	N'sheeka shel k'ravut ain ba g'nai. There is no shame in kissing your relatives.
Knowledge	332	Yir'at ha'shem, resheet da'at; chochma u'musar aveeleem bazu. Fear of the Lord is the beginning of knowledge; fools despise wisdom and morality.
	333	Yorseef da'at, yoseef machof The more knowledge, the more sorrow.

A 334 Gueersa d'yankuta la mishtakcha.
Knowledge obtained in childhood is not forgotten.

335 Ain lee elah she'anee yodai'a she'ainee yodai'a.
My chief merit is that I know that I don't know.

336 Hada'at cashemesh—v'hee tanees kol emesh.
Knowledge is like the sun—it dispels the darkness.

337 Raisheet da'at la'adam—da'at et atzmo.
Man's primary knowledge is self-knowledge.

338 Mee sherotzeh lada'at hakol mazken b'lo eeto.
Whoever wants to know everything, grows old prematurely.

L

Labor	339	Yagueeah capecha kee tocahl ashrecha, v'tov lach. If you eat the fruit of the labor of your hands, you'll prosper.
	A 340	Mita machamat mal'acha la shcheecha. Hard work never killed anyone.
	341	P'ameem sheha'avoda m'shana mazal. Sometimes labor will change your luck.
	Y 342	A mentsh ken essen alain ober er ken nit arebeiten alain. *A person can eat alone but he cannot labor alone.*
Ladder	343	Ha'olam domeh l'sulam: zeh oleh v'zeh yored. The world's like a ladder: one ascends, and one descends.
Land	344	Kol adam she'ain lo karka, aino adam. Every man who does not own land, is not a man.
	345	Adama she'aina ne'evedet doma l'eesha almana o galmuda. Land that is not worked is like a widow or a spinster.
Land of Israel	A 346	Aveera d'eretz yisrael machkeem. The air of the Land of Israel makes one wise.

Language	347	Kinor hapl'a'eem l'shon kol am. Every nation's language is like a miracle violin.
Laughter	348	Gam bischok yichav lev. Even in laughter, the heart aches.
	349	Eveel bitz'chok yareem kolo v'eesh arum b'nachat yihcayech. A fool raises his voice in laughter; a wise man smiles quietly.
	350	Lifnai elokeem, b'cheh; lifnai b'nai adam, tzchak. Weep before God; before people, laugh.
Lawyer	351	Prakleeteen shel adam—t'shuva u'ma'aseem toveem. A man's best lawyers are repentance and good deeds.
Lazy	352	Lech el n'mala atzel, r'eh dracheha vachacham. Go to the ant, sluggard; study its ways and become smart.
	353	Rabah b'adam atzlut hanefesh me'atzlut habasar. Laziness of the spirit is greater even than laziness of the flesh.
	354	Ha'atzlut ohevet l'hitztadek sh'aina osa clum mipnai sh'ain b'yicholta la'asot et hakol. Laziness likes to justify itself for not doing anything because it cannot do everything.
	355	Atzel mitivo ach charutz la'ootz. Some people are lazy by nature, and quick to give advice.
Leader	356	Oy lo latzibur she'hamanheeg she'lo hu am ha'aretz. Woe to the community whose leader is an ignoramus.
	357	Hamanheeg ha'ameetee shel hador tzareech sheyihiyeh kadosh. A generation's true leader must himself be saintly.

358 L'manheeg na'aseh al pee rov lo mee sheyodai'a
et haderech kee eem mee shesavur she'hu yodai'a
et haderech.
A leader is not necessarily one who knows the
way but one who thinks he knows the way.

Legend   **359** Agadot moshchot lev ha'adam cayayeen.
Legends, like wine, captivate people's hearts.

360 Siftotav shoshaneem—elu ha'agadot.
Legends are like rosy lips.

361 Agodatav shel am m'galot lanu et yofyo yoter
mishehu misgaleh b'ma'asai ha'am u'v'mikrav.
A people's legends reveal its character more
clearly than its acts and events.

Lending   **362** Eelu haya tov b'hash'eel kee az haya masheel
haba'al et ishto.
If lending were a good idea, then the husband
would lend out his wife.

363 Gadol hamalveh yoter min ha'oseh tzedaka.
He who lends money to the poor without
interest is greater than he who gives charity.

Lies   **364** Mid'var sheker tirchak.
Distance yourself from a lie!

365 V'tov rash me'eesh cazav.
Be a pauper, rather than a liar.

366 Cach onsho shel bada'ee: afeelu amar emet, ain
shom'een lo.
A liar's punishment—even when he tells the
truth, people don't believe him.

367 Lifameem gam hashakran y'daber emet.
Sometimes even the liar will speak the truth.

368 Hacazvan zeh darco she'yachshov she'culam caz-
vaneem camohu.
A liar believes everyone lies, just like him.

A 369   Shikra molled shikra.
One lie begets another.

Life   370   U'vachcarta bachayeem!
Choose life!

371   Chaval al heyotee bachayeem—u'fee me'ah al hedaree min hachayeem.
It's too bad about my life—and one hundred times worse if I had never lived.

372   Kelev chei yoter tov min aryeh met.
A live dog is better than a dead lion.

373   Y'mai shnotainu bahem shiveem shana, v'eem bigvurot, shmoneem.
The years of our life are seventy years, and sometimes by dint of strength eighty.

374   Achat hee lakol: derech m'vo hachayeem, u'motzaam.
For everyone, there is one entrance into life— and one exit.

A 375   Chayei, b'nai u'mzonai, la bizchuta talya milata ela b'mazala talya milata.
Length of life, children, sustenance—they depend not on merit, but on luck.

Light   376   Shlosha hema b'mordai ha'or: ganav, no'ef, v'atalef.
Three rebel against the light: the thief, the adulterer and the bat.

Lion   377   Aimat mafguee'a al ha'aree.
A lion is fearful of a gnat.

Lips   378   B'siftotav yilached rasha.
A wicked person will be trapped by his own lips.

Livelihood   379   Kasha parnasa k'kri'at yam suf.
Earning a living is as hard as splitting the Red Sea.

Logic	380	Ain hidur c'hidur higayon. There is no greater beauty than that of logic.
Lonely	381	Ain l'cha adam galmud yoter mimee she'ohev et atzmo. No person is lonelier than the one who loves himself.
	382	Boded hu ha'adam kol od lo matza et atzmo. A person is lonely until he finds himself.
Loss	383	Lo tireh et shor acheecha o et seyo nidacheem v'hitalamta mehem. Hashev t'sheevem l'acheecha. If you see your friend's ox or sheep straying, don't look the other way; return them to your friend.
Love	384	V'ahavta l're'echa camocha. You shall love your neighbor as yourself.
	385	Mayeem rabeem lo yuchlu l'chabot et ha'ahava u'n'harot lo yishtifuha. Many waters cannot quench love, nor can rivers drown it.
	386	Azah camabet ahava. Love is as strong as death.
	387	Anee l'dodee lee, v'dodee lee. My beloved is mine and I am his.
	388	Al kol p'sha'eem t'chaseh ahava. Love covers up all sins.
	389	Ha'ahava m'averet et ha'ainayeem mer'ot chesronot v'hasina m'averet ha'ainayeem mer'ot yitronot. Love blinds the eyes to faults, and hatred blinds the eyes to see virtues.
	390	Adam l'ahava nivra, v'eem sonai hu, l'cheenam hu chei. Man was born for love. If he hates, he was born in vain.

391 Ahava shlaima ainena.
Perfect love does not exist.

392 Rak ha'ahava mat'emet lanu ta'am nitzchiyut
b'toch chayai sha'a.
Only love gives us the taste of eternity.

393 Ahava y'shana vachasuda aina ma'ala caluda.
Old and true love does not rust.

394 Kol adam ohev, kulo same'ach.
A man in love is a happy man.

Luck 395 M'shaneh makom, m'shaneh mazal.
When you change your place (residence, job)
you change your luck for the better.

A 396 Mazala d'vai trai adeef.
Two together are luckier than one.

397 Mazal mach'keem, mazal ma'asheer.
Luck makes you wise, luck makes you wealthy.

398 Z'rok bar-mazal layam v'hu ya'aleh eem p'nina
b'yado.
Throw a lucky person into the sea, and he'll
emerge with a pearl in his hand.

Lust 399 O'y'vo shel adam—ta'avato.
A man's enemy is his lust.

400 Ta'ava m'vee'a leedai ahava.
Lust leads to love.

401 Achorai a'ree v'lo acharai eesha.
It's better to follow a lion than a woman.

Luxury 402 Haderech ha'yeshara hee ba'atzeerat kol
hamotarot.
The correct path is to give up all luxuries.

403 Bakashot hamotarot hen hamatreedot ha'adam
min halimud.
The demand for luxuries propel a person away
from studies.

M

Majority	404	Ain holcheen b'fiku'ach nefesh acharai harov. When a life is at stake, don't follow the majority.
	A 405	Tree udai yabeeshai v'chad rateeva, okeedan ya-beeshai l'rateeva. When there are two dry sticks, and one damp one, the dry will burn the damp.
	406	Al tet acharai rabeem lalechet nit'eh, kee lo rabeem yechk'mu. Don't follow the majority in the wrong path, because the majority are not always wise.
Man	407	Ain adam asher lo yecheta. There is no man who never sinned.
	408	Kol adam cozev. All men tell lies.
	409	Adam lahevel dama, yamav c'tzel over. Man is like a breath, his days like a passing shadow.
	410	Kol darchai eesh zach b'ainav All the ways of a man are pure in his own eyes.
	411	Elokeem asa et ha'adam yashar, v'hema bikshu chishvonot rabeem. God made man upright, but man searched out many crooked devices.

412 Ain tov la'adam tachat hashemesh kee eem
le'echol, lishtot v'lis'mo'ach.
Man has nothing good under the sun except to
eat, drink, and enjoy.

413 Da me'ayeen bata u'l'an ata holech.
Know where you came from and where you are
going.

414 Bishlosha d'vareem adam mishtaneh mechavero:
b'kol, b'mar'eh, u'v'da'at.
One man differs from another in three things:
his voice, his appearance, and his mind.

415 No'ach lo l'adam shelo nivra mishenivra.
It would have been better for a man not to have
been born than to have been born.

416 B'nai adam domeen l'isvai hasadeh, halalu notz-
itzin, v'halalu novleen.
People are like grass in the field: some blossom,
some wither.

417 Oy l'guever sanu lakol v'oy lee miguever ratzu'ee
lakol.
Woe to him who is hated by all, or to him who
is loved by all.

418 Ain chayot ra'ot, p'rat l'achat—ha'adam.
There are no bad beasts except one—man.

Manners *A* 419 Azalta l'karta halech b'nimusa.
When you're in a strange city, adopt its
manners.

420 Derech eretz kadma latorah.
Good manners supersede learning.

Marriage 421 Yoter mishe'eesh rotzeh lisa, eesha rotza
l'hinaseh.
More than a man wishes to wed, a woman
wishes to get married.

422   Esh v'eesha zachu—hashchina bainaihem. Lo
       zachu, esh ochlatam.
       If a man and his wife are deserving, God's pres-
       cence is with them; if they are not deserving,
       fire consumes them.

423   Yimkor adam kol ma sheyesh lo v'yisa bat tal-
       meed chacham—v'yasee bito l'talmeed chacham.
       A man should sell all he owns and marry a
       scholar's daughter—and marry off his daughter
       to a scholar.

424   Kol hamasee bito l'am ha'aretz, k'eelu kofta
       u'maneecha lifnai a'ree.
       Whoever marries off his daughter to a boor,
       it's as if he chained her and threw her before a
       lion.

425   Al tomar, ainee nosai eesha—elah sa eesha!
       Do not say "I will not get married"—get mar-
       ried!

426   Ain zivugo shel eesh elah min hakadosh baruch
       hu.
       A person's marriage partner comes from heaven.

427   Bitcha bagra, bo v'hasse'a!
       When your daughter matures, marry her off!

Master   428   Eem ha'adon nadeev, lo yihiyeh ha'eved kilei.
                     If the master is generous, the slave will not be
                     stingy.

Matchmaker   429   Mee she'aino m'shaker aino yachol lihiyot
                         shadchan.
                         Whoever cannot lie cannot be a matchmaker.

430   Kelev aino yachol lihiyot katzav, v'ravak aino
       yachol lihiyot shadchan.
       A dog can't be a butcher, and a bachelor can't be
       a matchmaker.

Meal	431	Habo'te'ach al se'udat chavero yisha'er b'lo se'uda. Whoever depends on eating at his friend's house will go hungry.
Measure for Measure	432	Elokeem m'chakeh z'man rav aval b'sofo shel davar m'shalem g'mul b'ribeet. God waits a long time, but pays back with interest.
	433	Kee ru'ach yizra'u v'sufata yiktzoru. They who sow the wind will reap the whirlwind.
	434	S'char mitzvah, mitzvah; s'char avaira, avaira. The reward for virtue is virtue; the reward for sin, is sin.
Medicine	435	Refu'ah m'tuka aina b'nimtza. There is no such thing as tasty medicine.
Memory	436	Zecher tzadeek livracha. The memory of a righteous person is a blessing.
	437	Lo kol hamarbeh bizcheera, machkeem. Not everyone with a good memory is intelligent.
Mending	438	K'shot atzm'cha, v'achar kach, k'shot achereem. First mend yourself, and then mend others.
Merchants	439	Derech hatagareen mar'een et hap'solet t'chila, v'achar kach mar'een hashevach. The merchant's way is first to show you junk, and then the good stuff.
Mercy	440	K'she'ain e'met, ain chesed. Without truth, there is no mercy.
	441	Bishveel hachesed ha'olam mitkayem. The world exists for the sake of mercy.
	442	Afeelu cherev chada munachat al tzavero shel adam, al yimna atzmo min harachameem. Even when a sharp sword rests on your neck, don't give up on mercy.

Messiah	443	Ain mashee'ach ba ad shetichleh ga'ava min ha'olam. The messiah will not come until pride disappears from the world.
Middle	444	Chayav adam l'halech b'emtza v'lo y'hai noteh l'chan v'lo l'chan. A person should walk down the middle of the path, and not veer to one side or the other.
Milk	445	Chalav eezeem sh'chorot v'chalav eezeem l'vanot echad hu. The milk of black goats and white goats is all the same.
Mind	446	Lev navon y'vakesh da'at. An intelligent mind will search for knowledge.
	447	Rishon sheba'ganaveem—gonev da'at habree'ot. The bigget thief is he who steals people's minds.
	448	Mitoch she'adam shaket, da'ato m'yushevet alav. When a man is at ease, so is his mind.
Miracle	449	Ain somcheen al hanes. One should not depend on miracles.
	450	Ma parnasa ee-efshar la'olam b'lo hee, kach ee-efshar la'olam b'lo niseem u'v'lo p'la'eem. Just as the world cannot exist without livelihoods, so it cannot exist without miracles and wonders.
Mirror	Y 451	Der shpiguel viezt ois dem emes. The mirror reveals the truth.
Miser	452	Al tilcham et lehem ra-ayeen; echol u'shtai yomar l'cha, v'libo bal imach. Don't eat a miser's bread; eat, drink, he says, but his heart is not in it.
	453	Mone'ah nafsho yikbotz l'acher, u'v'tovato yitba'bai'ah zar. He who denies himself amasses for others; a stranger will enjoy his wealth.

454   C'chol sheyit'asher hakilei, yarbeh kiluto.
        The richer a miser grows, the more his avarice
        expands.

455   Yoter tov l'hitchaber im am ha'aretz u'vatran
        b'mamono milihitchaber im talmeed chacham
        atzran v'kapdan.
        It's better to associate with a generous boor than
        with a stingy scholar.

Misfortune *A* 456   Tzara koret l'chaverta.
        One misfortune leads to another.

457   Eem tachat mipnai ha'ason lo tir'eh et ha'osher.
        If you always fear misfortune, you'll miss out on
        happiness.

458   Eesh nilbav c'alon chason rochev al asono.
        An intelligent person is like a strong oak: he
        rides over his misfortune.

Mistake   459   Mutav sheyihiyu shog'gueen v'al yihiyu
        m'zeedeen.
        It's better to err than to sin deliberately.

460   Yesh modeh al shig'gotav l'ma'an ha'alem z'dono-
        tav.
        Sometimes people admit their mistakes, to mask
        their crimes.

461   Yesh mishneh echad y'alefcha da'at yoter misheva
        mo'atzot.
        Occasionally one mistake is more instructive
        than seven advisers.

462   Kavod l'adam l'hodot al shguee'ah.
        It's an honor for a person to admit his mistake.

Modesty   463   Hadar chochma—anava.
        Modesty is wisdom's majesty.

464   Anava s'yag l'chochma.
        Modesty is a fence around wisdom.

465　Afeelu ata mushlam b'chol hamidot, eem ain
b'cha anava ata chaser.
Even if you are perfect in all virtues, if you're
not modest, you're wanting.

466　Kol tova m'oreret kina chutz meha'anava.
Every virtue arouses jealousy, except modesty.

467　G'dola anava mikol midot sheba'olam.
Modesty is the greatest virtue in the world.

468　Al yehaneh adam me'anv'tanuto.
A person should not derive pleasure from his
modesty.

469　Tz'nee'ut eesha—yofya.
A woman's beauty is her modesty.

Money　470　Adam bahul al mamono.
Money makes its owner frantic.

471　Ohev kesef lo yisba kesef.
Whoever loves money will never be satisfied
with how much he has.

472　Kesef m'taher mamzereem.
Even bastards are purified by money.

473　Kol she'hakesef b'yado, yado al ha'elyona.
Whoever has cash in hand, he has the upper
hand.

474　B'tzel hachochma, b'tzel hakesef.
Where there is money, there is wisdom.

Y 475　Tzuleeb guelt iz die velt guevoren mees.
Because of money, the world became ugly.

476　Hakesef hu adon kasheh v'gam eved tov
v'charutz.
Money is a hard taskmaster; it is also a good,
diligent servant.

Moral 477 Sifrai musar yesh lanu de v'hoter aval anshai
musar kol cach m'at.
We have plenty of morality books, but so few
moral people.

478 Hamusar v'hayofee hem zeheem b'ikaram.
Morality and beauty are essentially the same.

Mother 479 Al tavuz kee zakna eemecha.
Do not despise your mother when she is old.

480 Elokeem aino yachol lihiyot b'chol makom,
lachen bara imahot.
Since God could not be everywhere, He created
mothers.

Y 481 Siz nit da aza zach vee a shlechte muter tzu a
guten toit.
There is no such thing as a bad mother or a
good death.

Mother-in- 482 Adam haya ham'ushar ba'anasheem: lo hayeta
Law lo chotenet.
Adam was the luckiest of men: he had no
mother-in-law.

Mourner 483 Hakol holcheem l'vait ha'avel, v'chol echad
bocheh al tza'aro.
We all visit the mourner, but we weep for our
own misfortune.

Mouth 484 Notzer peev, shomer nafsho.
The one who guards his mouth, preserves his
life.

485 B'fee k'seeleem libam u'v'lev chachameem pee-
hem.
The hearts of fools are in their mouths but the
mouths of the wise are in their hearts.

N

Naked	486	Al ta'amod arom lifnai haner. Do not stand nude before the candlelight.
	487	Ervat hachachameem bain raglaihem, v'ervat hak'seel bain l'chayav. The wise man's nakedness is between his loins, and that of the fool between his cheeks.
Name	488	Tov shem tob mishemen tov. A good name is better than (precious) oil.
	489	Hashem hu etzem hanefesh shel ha'adam. His name is the very soul of a man.
Nation	490	Ee efshar l'adam pratee lihiyot adam kol zman she'amo chaya torefet. It's not possible for a person to be a genuine individual so long as his people is like a wild beast.
Nature	491	Ain kera bateva. There is no chasm in nature.
	492	Tivo shel olam aino mishtaneh. The nature of the world doesn't change.
Near	493	Lo kol harov karov v'lo kol harachok rachok. Not everything nearby is near, and not everything faroff is far.
Necessity	494	Hahechrach lo yeshubach v'lo yegueneh. Necessity is not to be praised nor shamed.

495 Hahecrach barzel yaro'ach.
Necessity can splinter iron.

Neck 496 Bihiyot hatzavar lavan, ain tzorech la'anak.
If your neck is white, you don't need a necklace.

Need 497 Tzorchai amcha m'rubeem.
The people's needs are great.

Y 498 Ven dein noit iz grois, vos nointer iz Gott.
The greater your need, the closer is God.

Needle 499 Hamachat, katan v'dak, viyichalkel guever
uvaito.
The needle, small and thin, can support a man
and his family.

Neighbor 500 V'ahavta l'rai'echa camocha.
Love your neighbor as yourself.

501 Tov shachen karov me'ach rachok.
A close neighbor is better than a distant brother.

502 Al yicanes adam pitom l'vait chavero.
Never enter your neighbor's house suddenly.

503 Ee efshar l'hasteer shum davar me'elokeem o
me'hashachen.
You can't hide anything from God—or from a
neighbor.

New 504 V'yashan mipnai chadash totzee'u.
Clear out the old, make room for the new.

News 505 Ain kol chadash tachat hashemesh.
There is nothing really new under the sun.

506 Mayeem kareem al nefesh ayaifa u'shmu'a tova
mai'eretz merchak.
Like cold water to a tired soul, so is good news
from a distant land.

Night 507 Haleilah nivra lachashov bo ma'aseh hayom.
Night was created so that we might consider
what we did during the day.

| Noise | *A* 508 | Istera b'lagueena 'kish, kish' karya. |
| | | A penny in a box rattles the most. |

| Nurse | 509 | Aina domah omenet l'em. |
| | | A nurse is different from a mother. |

O

Oath	510	Lishvu'a al t'lamed peecha. Do not grow accustomed to uttering oats.
	511	Ain adam moreesh shvu'a l'vanav. A man cannot bequeath an oath to his sons.
	512	Eem ganavta, sofcha l'hishava lashaker. If you steal, eventually you'll commit perjury.
	513	Shvu'at shav—chilul ha'shem. A false oath desecrates God's name.
Occupation	514	Aizohee ha'avoda ha'r'tzu'a l'adam b'yoter? Zo shela hu mat'eem b'yoter. Which is a man's most desirable occupation? The one for which he is most fit.
Office	515	L'eeteem lo hamisra osa et ha'adam elah ha'adam oseh et hamisra. Sometimes the position does not make the man, but the man makes the position.
	516	Afeelu kal she'b'kaleem v'nismana parnas al hatzibur, haraihu k'abeer she'b'abeereem. Even the least worthy of men is named head of the community, he soars and becomes the mightiest of men.
Old	517	Mipnai saiva takoom v'hadarta pnai zaken. Rise before the old, show respect to the aged.

518   Al tashlichenu l'et zikna.
Do not abandon us when we grow old.

519   B'sheesheem chochma.
At sixty years of age, we achieve wisdom.

520   Al t'vayesh enosh yasheesh kee nimaneh mizkeneem.
Don't shame an oldster, for we'll all be counted among them.

A 521   Sava b'vaita, pach b'vaita, savta b'vaita, seema.
An old man in the house is a curse; an old woman, a blessing.

522   Da'atan shel z'keneem mishtanot.
As men age, their views change.

523   Hazikna em hashichecha.
Old age is the mother of forgetfulness.

Y 524   Ver ibergait zeine tzoris in a hundert yohr, vet leben lang.
Whoever master his troubles in one hundred years, will live along.

Opinion   525   K'shem she'ain partzufai b'nai adam domeem, kach ain dai'otaihem domot.
Just as people's faces are different, so are their opinions different.

526   Hadai'ot hem b'tzimtzum v'chilukai dai'ot b'shefa.
Opinions are scanty, but differences of opinion abound.

Optimism   527   Gam zo l'tova!
This too is for the best!

Orphan   528   Hamegadel yatom v'itoma b'toch baito, k'eelu y'ladam.
Whoever rears orphans in his home, it is as though he/she gave birth to them.

529   M'acher lakachat lo eesha, m'maher la'azov ye-
tomeem.
When the orphans rejoice, heaven and earth join
them.

Whoever takes a wife late, leaves orphans early.

530   K'she'hayetomeem s'mecheem, shamayeem
va'aretz imam mishtatfeem.
When the orphans rejoice, heaven and earth join
them.

P

Paradise   531   Kol ma she'bara hakadosh baruch hu bara
k'negdo: Bara gan eden, bara gaihinom.
For everything He created, God created an
opposite: a paradise, a hell.

532   Gam b'zeh ha'olam yesh l'haseeg ta'anug gan
eden.
Even in this world, one can taste the joy of paradise.

533   Yesh r'u'yeem b'ad mach'sh'votaihem gan eden
u'v'ad ma'asaihem l'gaihinom.
There are people who deserve paradise for their
thoughts, and hell for their deeds.

534   Gan eden kayam b'chol makom l'gabai deedo
shel hayehudi hama'meen.
Paradise exists everywhere for the true believers.

Parents   535   Ma she'elokeem hu la'olam, horeem hem
l'yaldaihem.
What God is to the world, parents are to their
children.

536   Eem lo t'chabed horecha, lo y'chabducha
banecha.
If you don't respect your parents, your children
will not respect you.

537   Av va'em lo koneem b'chesef.
You cannot acquire parents with money.

Partners	538	Zeh yachazeek et hapara b'karneha, v'hashenee motzee chalav me'ateeneha. One holds the cow by her horns, and the other one milks her.
	539	B'makom she'hashutafeem m'rubeem, hat'anot m'rubot. The more partners, the more arguments.
	Y 540	Shitfis iz guit nor mit dein froi, un aintzegueh zog'n az dos iz oich nit zeecher. Partnership is good only with your wife—and there are those who say this too is not certain.
Past	541	Hatzo'ek lishe'avar, harai zeh t'filat shav. Whoever is crying for the past is praying in vain.
	542	Ain hayacheed yachol l'hibanot blee shum ke-sher im he'avar. No individual can be whole without some link to the past.
	543	He'avar manee'ach pasai barzel bishveel he'ateed. The past puts down a railroad track for the future.
	544	Ateedo shel am ba'avaro. A nation's future lies in its past.
Patience	545	Erech apayeem rav-t'vuna, uk'tzar ru'ach mereem ivelet. A person slow to anger has great understanding; one with a quick temper exalts foolishness.
	546	Tov erech ru'ach mi'g'va ru'ach. One who is patient in spirit surpasses one who is proud in spirit.
	547	Kol mee she'hu savlan yihiyeh adon. A patient person will become a moster.
	548	Hasavlanut—machatzeet hayedee'a. Patience is already half-way to knowledge.

Pay   *A* 549   Ee agra, la fagra—v'ee fagra la agra.
                       If you receive pay, you cannot sit idle; and if
                       you sit idle, you cannot receive pay.

Peace   550   V'haya ma'aseh hatzedaka shalom.
                       The reward for righteousness is peace.

            551   Kee achareet l'eesh shalom.
                       There is a future for a man of peace.

            552   Talmeedai chachameem marbeen shalom ba'olam.
                       Scholars expand peace in the world.

            553   Kol yehudee she'ain lo eesha sharu'ee b'lo sha-
                       lom.
                       A Jew without a wife will not find peace in this
                       life.

            554   Shalom blee emet hu shlom shav.
                       Peace without truth is a false peace.

            555   Hashalom chashuv min ha'emet.
                       Peace matters more than truth.

            556   Shalom lo yakum b'ezrat ko'ach elah mitoch ha-
                       vana.
                       Peace wil not rise by force, but only through un-
                       derstanding.

            557   Eem lo timtza hashalom b'kirb'cha, shav ta'amol
                       l'matzehu b'makom acher.
                       If you can't find peace within you, you'll labor
                       in vain to find it elsewhere.

Pedigree 558   Hachochma hee hayichus hagadol.
                       Wisdom is the greatest pedigree.

            559   Ach shav hithalelcha bichvod bait aveecha, eem
                       lo yuchlu hit'halel b'cha yotz'ai chalatzecha.
                       It's vain to flaunt your father's pedigree if your
                       children don't take pride in you.

Pen   560   Hakulmus—shlee'ach halev.
                       The pen is the envoy of the heart.

561 Sechel ha'eesh hu tachat chudo shel ha'et.
A man's intelligence is located in the tip of the
pen.

Penny 562 Kol pruta u'fruta mitztarefet l'cheshbon gadol.
Pennies add up to a sizable total.

People 563 Mah yomru habree'ot?
What will people say?

564 Kol hamon, c'kol shadei.
The voice of the people is like the voice of the
Almighty.

565 Yesh kol meenai bree'ot ba'olam: chamoreem
u'fradot, klaveem v'chazeereem, v'gam tola'eem.
There are all kinds of people in the world:
asses and mules, dogs and hogs, ad also worms.

Perfect Y566 Tzu zein does feinste and beste—dos alain iz a
chisaron.
To strive for and achieve perfection—that
alone is a fault.

Perfume 567 Shemen u'k'toret yisamach lev.
Oil and perfume gladden the heart.

Perseverance 568 Sheva yipol tzadeek vakam.
A righteous man falls seven times and rises
again.

569 Hahatmada hee m'kor hasechel v'hachochma.
Perseverance is the source of intelligence and
wisdom.

570 Ha'adam nimshal latzipor: b'chocha shel tzipor
la'alot mala, mala, bitnei shetanee'a et k'nafeha
blee heref.
Man is like a bird: a bird can fly higher and
higher, but only if its wings continue to move
without stopping.

Pessimism	571	Pessimist hu adam she'b'sha'a shema'ameedeem oto bain shtai ra'ot, haraihu bocher bishtaihen. A pessimist, confronted with two bad choices, chooses both.
	572	Haderech hatova she'yavor lo adam: pessimiyut b'ha'aracha v'optimiyut b'ma'aseh. The best way for a man to choose is pessimism in appraisal and optimism in action.
Philosophy	573	B'chol dor vador nitvasefet da'at shel pilusufeeya, uva'ot chochmot chadashot, v'al y'day zeh mitchadsheem choloyeem rabeem b'chol dor. In every generation there is more knowledge of philosophy, and new wisdoms arise—thus new illnesses are added to every generation.
Pillow	Y 574	Ah driter tor nit arein krichen tz'vishen tzvai vos shlofen oif ain kish'n. A third party may not interfere between two who sleep on the same pillow.
Pious	575	Chaseed shoteh v'rasha arum v'eesha prusha: harai elu m'chalai olam. A stupidly devout man, the slyly evil, and the sanctimonious woman—these will destroy the world.
Pity	576	Kol efshar lo l'vakesh rachameem al chavero v'aino m'vakesh, nikra choteh. Whoever can ask pity for his friend, but doesn't do so, he is called a sinner.
	577	Midat hachemla yesod gadol v'chazak l'tikun hamidot. Pity is a great, strong foundation for improving your character.
	578	Harachmanut hee shoresh shel habree'a. Pity is a root of all creation.
Place	579	Ain l'cha davar she'ain lo makom. Every single thing has a place of its own.

Plant	580	Et lata'at v'et la'akor natu'a. There is a time to plant, and a time to harvest.
Pleasure	581	B'nee, eem yesh l'cha sharet nafsh'cha, z'chor kee lo bish'ol ta'anug. My son, do as much good as you can.... remember, there is no joy in the nether world.
	582	Eesh machsor ohev simcha. He who loves pleasure shall be a poor man.
	583	Shibachtee et hasimcha, asher ain tov la'adam tachat hashemesh kee eem le'echol v'lishtot v'lismo'ach. I commended pleasure for man has nothing good under the sun other than to eat, drink and be merry.
Pocket	Y 584	Der veg tzu a mentsh's keshene iz gueferlech grois. The way to a man's pocket is terribly long.
	585	Adam karov l'cheeso. A man is related to his pocket.
Poetry	586	Ham'shor'reem hem halev v'nefesh shel ha'am. Poets are the heart and soul of a people.
	587	Hatov shebasheereem hu ma sheda'at bnai aliya nocha haimena v'hehamon meveen ota. The best of poems is that which intelligent people are content with, and ordinary people understand them.
Police	588	Eem y esh shotreem, yesh shofteem; eem ain shotreem, ain shofteem. If there are police, there are judges; if there are no police, there are no judges.
Poor	589	Kee yamuch acheecha, v'hechezakta bo. If your brother becomes poor, support him.
	590	Ain anee elah b'dai'a. The only poor man is a simpleton.

591　Galgal hu shechozer ba'olam.
　　　The wheel (of poverty) is ever-revolving.

592　Ha'onee v'hazikna rochveem tzmudeem.
　　　Poverty and old age often travel together.

Y 593　Orimkeit iz nit kein beesha, ober darfst nit
　　　shtoltzirin mit im.
　　　Poverty is no disgrace, but neither do you have
　　　to take pride in it.

Y 594　Az an arumer est a hun, oder er iz krank tze der
　　　hun iz.
　　　When a pauper eats a chicken, either he is—or
　　　the chicken was.

Postpone　595　D'cheeya goreret d'cheeya.
　　　One postponement leads to another.

Power of　596　Hagaru'a bivnai adam hu mee sheco'ach
Speech　　　l'shono oleh al co'ach sichlo.
　　　The worst kind of person is one whose power
　　　of speech is greater than his power of thought.

Praise　597　Yihalelcha zar, v'lo peecha.
　　　Let a stranger praise you—but not your own
　　　mouth.

598　Omreem miktzat shivcho shel adam b'fanav,
　　　v'chulo shelo b'fanav.
　　　Tell part of a man's praise to his face, but behind
　　　his back tell it all.

599　L'fee bigdo yehulal eesh b'vo'o, u'l'fee sichlo
　　　b'tzeto.
　　　A man is praised when he enters according to
　　　his appearance, and according to his wit when
　　　he departs.

Prayer　600　Hamashmee'a kolo bitfilato, harai zeh
　　　miktannai amana.
　　　Whoever prays loudly, it shows he has little
　　　faith.

601 Sha'arai t'fila ainam ninaleem me'olam.
The gates of prayer are never locked.

602 Mutav t'fila blee bait knesset mibait knesset blee t'fila.
Prayer without a synagogue is preferred to a synagogue without prayer.

603 T'filat tzadeekeem k'tzara.
The prayer of the righteous is brief.

Precept 604 Shomer mitzva, shomer nafsho.
Whoever keeps a commandment, preserves his life.

605 Eekar hamitzvot l'yasher halev.
The chief purpose of the precepts is to straighten the heart.

Pregnant 606 He'hara mishtokeket l'sheleg kalu'ee.
A pregnant woman longs for toasted snow.

Present 607 Hahoveh tzareech tameed l'shalem m'cheer he'ateed.
The present must always pay the price of the future.

Pride 608 Al tihee gavchan bilshonecha.
Don't be filled with pride or boasting when you speak.

609 Lifnai shever gaon v'lifnai kishalon gova ru'ach.
Pride goes before destruction, and a haughty spirit before a fall.

610 N'see'eem v'ru'ach v'gueshem ayeen—eesh mit'halel b'matat sheker.
Like clouds and winds without rain is a man who boasts of gifts he does not give.

611 Ga'avat adam tashpilenu.
A man's pride will bring him low.

612   Ain l'cha ga'ava m'guna mishel mee shemisga'eh
       b'anv'tanuto.
       There is no worse pride than that of the man
       who boasts of his modesty.

Profit   613   Harevach v'hahefsed chavereem.
                     Profit and loss are companions.

Promise   614   Hayotzeh mipeechem ta'asu!
                     Do what you promised!

Proof   615   Hamotzee mechavero alav har'aya.
                     The burden of proof is on the plaintiff.

              616   Hamefursamot ainan tzreechot r'aya.
                     Well-known things do not need proof.

Prophet   Y 617 Der nar iz a halber novee.
                     The fool is a half-prophet.

              618   Ain navee b'eero.
                     No man is a prophet in his own town.

Protest   A 619 K'var tzvachu kama'ai d'kamach.
                     Long before you, elders also protest.

              620   Kol mee sheyesh b'yado limchot v'aino
                     mocheh, ne'enash alav.
                     Whoever can protest against a wrong, and does
                     not, will be punished.

Proverb   621   Divrai chachameem cadarvonot.
                     The sayings of the wise are like goads.

              622   Al y'dai hameshaleem yored ha'adam l'omek
                     hadevareem.
                     A person can understand things deeply through
                     proverbs.

              623   Hamichtav hatov c'yahalom yivade'a, mefeetz
                     noga af pole'ach u'voke'a.
                     A pointed proverb is like a diamond: it emits
                     light, and it also cuts.

624   Lifameem timtza et hapilusufeeya shel ha'am
       k'she'hee s'funa bapitgameem.
       At times you'll find a people's outlook in its prov-
       erbs.

625   Ain pitgam cozev.
       No proverb is untrue.

Public   626   Ain hayacheed yachol la'amod bifnai hatzibur.
                     No individual can stand up to the whole
                     community.

Punish   627   Ain onsheen elah eem ken mazheereen.
                     Do not punish without first giving warning.

628   Ha'onasheem lachot'eem ainam b'torat n'kama.
       Punishment of the sinner should not be seen as
       revenge.

629   V'aseeta lo ca'asher zamam la'asot l'acheev.
       Do to him as he schemed to do to his fellow
       man.

Pupil   630   Talmeedo shel adam nikra b'no.
                    A man's pupil is like his own son.

631   Ain harav mitkaneh b 'talmeedo.
       No teacher envies his own pupil.

632   Lo habeishan lomed.
       A shy person does not learn.

633   Lo hakapdan m'lamed.
       A rigid person cannot teach.

634   Harbeh lamad'tee merabotei u'mechaverei, umi-
       talmeedei yoter mikuam.
       I learned much from my teachers, more from
       my friends, and the most from my pupils.

Q

Quality	*A* 635	Kaba me'ara v'la kora me'igara. It's better to have a little close by than a lot far away.
	636	Gam avatee'ach v'gam adam kasheh la'amod mi-yad al teevam. It's hard to know the quality of a person, or a watermelon.
Quarrel	637	Kavod l'eesh shevet mereev. It's an honor for a man to desist from a quarrel.
	638	B'kerev anasheem nitzeem al teshev, kee achareet matza katel. Don't dwell among the quarrelsome; dissension leads to murder.
	639	Acharai kol k'tata—charata. After every quarrel—remorse.
	640	Kol ha'oseh m'reeva im rabo, c'oseh im shcheena. Whoever quarrels with his teacher, it's as though he did so with God.
Question	641	She'ailat hechacham chatzee hachochma. A sage's question is like half the answer.
	642	Lo kol she'aila r'uya litshuva. Not every question deserves an answer.

643 Lo titbayesh k'she'sho'aleem mimcha ma shelo yadata, lomar: ainee yode'a.
When you're asked a question and don't know the answer, don't be embarrassed to say, I don't know.

Quiet 644 Tov pat chareva v'shalva ba, mibayeet maleh zivcheh reev.
A dry crust of bread is better in a quiet house than a house full of feasting and strife.

645 Hashalva hee hagdola baneemot.
Peace and quiet are the greatest delights.

646 Tov m'lo caf nachat mimlo chofneiyeem amal u'r'ut ru'ach.
A handful of quiet is better than both hands jammed with oil, and striving after wind.

Quotation 647 Pasuk bizmano k'nahama bish'at ra'ava.
A quotation at the right moment is like bread to the hungry.

R

Rabbi   648   Harav aino elah yodai torah—aval aino hatorah atzma.
The rabbi is just the man who knows Torah—he is not the Torah itself.

Rage   649   Al tivahel b'ruchacha lichos, kee ka'as b'chaik k'seeleem yanuach.
Don't be quick to get angry; rage is found in the bosom of fools.

Rain   650   Aizehu yom shekol ha'olam shaveem? K'sheha'g'shameem yordeem.
When is the whole world equal? When the rain falls.

651   Eem ain eretz, ain matar. Eem ain matar, ain eretz. V'eem ain shnaihem, ain adam.
No land, no rain. No rain, no land. Without both, no mankind.

Reason   *A* 652   La b'savai ta'ama, v'la b'dard'dai etza.
You can't find reason with the aged, nor can you counsel with them.

Rebuke   653   Al tochach letz pen yisna'echa, hochach l'chacham v'ye'eh'haveka.
Do not rebuke one who scorns, lest he hate you; rebuke a wise man, and he will love you.

654   Soneh tochachat—ba'ar.
Whoever hates a reprimand is stupid.

655 Tova tochachat m'gula me'ahava m'suteret.
Better a public rebuke than unrevealed love.

656 Hatochacha m'vee'a leedai ahava.
A rebuke can lead to love.

Reciprocity 657 Shomr lee va'eshmor l'cha.
Look after me, and I'll look after you.

Recovery 658 Choleh ha'omed mechalyo chozer lee'mai alumav.
A patient, when he recovers, returns to his youthful days.

Redemption 659 Mah parnasa b'chol yom, af g'ula b'chol yom.
Like a livelihood, redemption must be earned each day.

660 Hag'ula ha'ateeda tihiyeh b'otzem plee'ata mimeen bree'a.
The future eredemption will be as marvelous as was Creation.

Religion 661 Ain dat eem ahavat betza.
It cannot be true religion if it loves money.

662 Hamedina m'chayevet v'chofa, hadat mora u'm'shadelet; hamedina notenet chukeem, v'hadat—mitzvot.
The state compels and coerces, religion teaches and persuades; the state enacts laws, religion proffers religious commandments.

663 Hadat, c'mo lashon, hee meta ca'asher paska l'hishtanot.
Religion, like a language, is dead when it stops changing.

664 Ain dat muchletet.
There is no absolute religion.

665   Kol ha'omer l'taken et hadat, harai hu b'ainei
k'eelu omer l'karer et ha'esth.
Whoever says he will repair religion, in my
eyes it's like somone who says he'll cool the fire.

666   B'et chet, aseh t'shuva.
While sinning, repent!

667   Rabee Eliezer omer: Shuv yom echad lifnai
mitatcha.
Rabbi Eliezer says: Repent one day before your
death.

668   Yafa sha'a achat bitshuva u'ma'aseem toveem
ba'olam hazeh mikol chayai ha'olam haba.
Better one hour of repentance and good deeds
in this world than a lifetime in the world to
come.

669   T'shuva m'chaperet al avairot kalot.
Repentance atones for minor sins.

670   Eem haya baal-t'shuva lo yomar lo, "Z'chor
ma'asecha rishoneem."
Don't say to a penitent: "Remember what you
once did."

671   Tachleet chochma t'shuva u'ma'aseem toveem.
Wisdom's goal is repentance and good deeds.

672   Sha'arai t'shuva l'olam p'tucheem.
The gates of repentance are eternally open.

673   Eem adam oseh t'shuva v'chozer la'avairotav, ain
zo t'shuva.
If a man repents, and then reverts to sinning—
that's not repentance.

674   Hatshuva l'chot'eem car'fu'a latachalu'eem.
Repentance for the sinners is like medicine for
the sick.

Respect	675	Harav shemachal al k'vodo, k'vodo machul. A teacher who surrenders the respect due him is no longer respected.
Responsibility	676	Ha'eesh echad yechta, v'al kol ha'eda tiktzof? If one congregant sins, is the whole congregation responsible?
	677	Adam mu'ad l'olam: bain shog'eg, bain mezeed, bain er, bain yashen. A person is always responsible: if his act was acci- dental or intentional, whether he was awake or asleep.
	678	Ben lo yisa ba'avon ha'av, v' ha'av ba'avon ha'ben. A son shall not suffer for a father's sin, nor vice versa.
	679	Ain adam nitpas bish'at tza'aro. A person is not responsible for an act committed in his time of distress.
Reward	680	Al tihiyu ca'avadeem hamesham'sh'meem et harav al m'nat l'kabel pras elah she'lo l'kabel pras. Don't be like servants who serve the master in order to win a prize but do it without expecting a reward.
Rich	681	Bote'ach b'oshro, hu yipol. Whoever trusts in his riches will fall.
	682	Ohavai asheer rabeem. A rich man has many admirers.
	683	Atz l'ha'asheer lo yinakeh. Whoever hastens to grow rich will not go unpun- ished.
	684	Marbeh n'chaseem, marbeh d'aga. The more riches, the more worries.
	685	Aizehu asheer? Hasame'ach b'chelko. Who is rich? He who is happy with his station in life.

Y686   Die reicher esen nit gold un die orimer esen nit
       shtainer.
       The rich don't eat gold, and the poor don't eat
       stones.

Righteous   687   Tzadeek avad v'ain eesh sam al lev.
                  A righteous person dies, and no one takes it to
                  heart.

       688   Na'ar hayeetee gam zakantee v'lo ra'eetee tzadeek
             ne'ezav v'zar'o m'vakesh lechem.
             I was young, now I'm old, and I did not see a
             righteous man forsaken and his children begging
             for bread.

       689   Pee tzadeek yanuv chochma.
             The mouth of a righteous person is a fount of
             wisdom.

       690   Tzadeek catamar yifrach, ca'erez balevanon yis-
             gueh.
             A righteous man will thrive like a palm tree;
             he'll grow like a cedar in Lebanon.

       691   Al t'hee tzadeek harbeh!
             Don't be too righteous!

       692   Tzadeekeem omreem m'at v'oseem harbeh.
             The righteous say little and do much.

       693   Et hakol ra'eetee bi mai chevlee: yesh tzadeek
             oved b'tzidko v'yesh rasha ma'areech b'ra'ato.
             In my life of vanity I saw everything: a righteous
             man dying in his righteousness, and a wicked
             man living long after his evil deeds.

       694   Kee adam ain tzadeek ba'aretz asher ya'aseh tov
             v'lo yecheta.
             There is not a righteous man on earth who does
             only good and doesn't sin.

       695   Bishveel tzadeek echad ha'olam nivra.
             Even for only one righteous person the world
             would have been created.

696 Kol mee shesoneh et hatzadeekeem, k'eelu soneh
et hamakom.
All those who hate the righteous, it's as though
they despise God.

Rivalry 697 Kin'at sofreem tarbeh chochma.
The rivalry of scholars increases wisdom.

698 Ain shnai zarzeereem yeshaineem al daf echad.
Two starlings do not sleep on the same perch.

River 699 Kol hanechalelem holcheem el hayam v'hayam
ainenu malai.
All streams run to the sea, but the sea is not full.

A 700 Nahara, nahara u'g'shatai.
Every river has its own course.

Root 701 Hateva noten sheyimsh'lu hashorasheem
ba'anafeem.
Nature's way is for a tree's roots to rule over its
leaves.

Rope *A* 702 Ishterai chad chevel, ishterai train chavaleem.
Untying one of two ropes tied together means
you untie both.

703 Chevel shenimtach harbeh alul l'hikare'a.
A rope too tightly drawn is apt to tear.

Rose 704 Nit'ater g'vee'ari v'radeem b'terem yibolu.
Let us adorn ourselves with roses before they
wither.

705 Eem lilkot shoshaneem iveeta, al tira pen yikov
cho'ach apecha.
If you want to pick roses, do not fear the thorns
will prick you.

Rule 706 Eem ba'a halacha tachat yadecha v'ain ata
yodai'a ma teeva, al tafliguena l'davar acher.
If you find a ruling whose meaning you don't
understand, don't divert it to something else.

707   Halacha she'hee rofefet b'vait deen v'ain ata yo-
        daia ma teeva, tze u'reh aich hatzibur noheg,
        un'n'hog.
        The rules that prevail in a courtroom, you don't
        know why, go and see how the public behaves,
        and act accordingly.

S

Sabbath	708	Kol s'fek nefashot docheh et hashabbat. Where life is in danger, Sabbath laws do not apply.
	709	Shabbat hee achat misheesheem la'olam haba. Sabbath has about it a flavor of paradise.
	710	Yoter mi'yisra'el shamra et hashabbast, shamra hashabbat otam. More than the Jewish people preserved the Sabbath, the Sabbath preserved them.
Salt	711	Kol hak'dairot tzreechot melach, v'ain kol hak'dairot tzreechot tavleen. All dishes need salt, but they don't all need spices.
Satan	712	Hu satan, hu yetzer hara. Put another way, Satan is a person's wish to do evil.
	713	Hasatan yachol la'avor derech kof hamachat. Satan can slip in through the eye of a needle.
Saving	714	Kovetz al yad yarbeh. He who amasses a little at a time will build a nest egg.
	715	Tova pruta shechasachta mishekel shehirvachta. A penny saved is better than a coin you earned.

| Scholar | 716 | Hevai mitabek ba'afar raglai chachameem v'hevai shoteh b'tzama et divraihem. |
| | | Sit in the dust at the feet of scholars, and drink in their words thirstily. |

| | 717 | Talmeedai chachameem marbeem shalom ba'olam. |
| | | Scholars enhance peace in the world. |

| | 718 | Eshet talmeed chacham harai hee c'talmeed chacham. |
| | | A scholar's wife is regarded as one too. |

| | 719 | Aizehu talmeed chacham? Kol she'sho'aleen oto halacha b'chol makom v'omra. |
| | | Who is a scholar? One who can interpret questions of law at any time, anywhere. |

| | 720 | Talmeedai chachameem, kol zman she-mazkeeneem, chochma nitosefet bahem. |
| | | The older scholars become, the wiser they become. |

| | 721 | Ain adam nolad lamdan. |
| | | No person is born a scholar. |

| School | 722 | Mutar la'asot mibait haknesset bait midrash. |
| | | It is permissible to transform a synagogue into a school, but not the other way around. |

| | 723 | Kol eer she'ain ba tinokot shel bait raban, machareeveem ota. |
| | | A city without school children is doomed to destruction. |

| Science | 724 | Hamada blee dat tzole'a, hadat blee mada iveret. |
| | | Science without religion is lame, religion without science is blind. |

| Seal | 725 | Chotamo shel hakadosh baruch hu emet. |
| | | Truth is the seal of God. |

| Secret | 726 | Masteer sod, ohev c'nafesh. |
| | | Whoever keeps a secret is a bosom friend. |

727 Galeh sod'cha l'echad me'elef.
Disclose your secret to only one in a thousand.

728 Nichnas yayeen, yatza sod.
When wine goes in, the secret goes out.

729 Hasod bain shneiyeem; v'sod hashlosha aino sod.
A secret is between two; when a third is involved, it's no secret.

730 Ain sod b'nasheem.
Women don't know what a secret is.

Self-control **731** Aizehu guibor? Hakovesh et yitzro.
Who's a hero? He who masters his impulses.

Self-Help **732** Eem am aino yacho la'azor l'atzmo, lo notar ma la'asot.
If a people can't help itself, they can't be helped at all.

733 Eem ain anee lee, ain gam ata lee.
If I'm not for myself, you won't be either.

734 Eem ain anee lee mee lee? U'ch'she'anee l'atzmee, ma anee? V'eem lo achshav, aimatei?
If I am not for myself, who will be? But if I am only for myself, what am I? And if not now, then when?

Sentiment **735** Ma she'ya'aseh hareguesh, lo ya'aseh hasechel.
What the emotions can do, brains cannot.

Shame **736** Lo yodai'a a'val boshet.
An unjust man does not know shame.

737 Hamalbeen pnai chavero barabeem k'eelu shofech dameem.
Whoever shames his friend in public is like one who sheds blood.

738 Bushata shel eesha m'ruba mishel eesh.
A woman's shame is greater than that of a man.

Shoe	739	Ain min'al echad oleh yafeh l'chol haraglayeem. No one shoe fits every foot.
Shroud	740	Ain keeseem batachreecheem. There are no pockets in shrouds.
Sick	741	Hamevaker choleh notel echad mishishim b'tza'aro. Whoever visits a sick friend lessens his pain a little.
	742	Cholee hanefesh kasheh micholee hagoof. Sickness of the spirit is worse than sickness of the flesh.
	743	K'she'hacholeh noteh lamut, m'naseem harof'eem gam et hatrufot hayoter m'supakot v'hayoter m'sukanot. When a sick person looks like he is dying, the doctors experiment with the most doubtful and dangerous medicines.
Sigh	744	Anacha shoveret chatzee gufo shel adam. A sigh can shatter a person's body.
Silence	745	Mee yiten hacharesh tacharishun, u't'hee lachem l'chochma. If only you remained silent—that would be your wisdom.
	746	Et lachashot v'et l'daber. There is a time to be silent, and a time to speak.
	747	Yafa shteeka lachachameem, kal vachomer latipsheem. Silence is good for the wise, and even more so for the fools.
	748	Hashteeka tova min hata'ut. Silence is better than making an error.
	749	Hashteeka hee ee mutzak b'lev yam roguesh mileem. Silence is a strong island in a sea throbbing with words.

Simple	750	Lihiyot tameem, zo ma'ala bainoneet; ulam, l'hatmeed bitmeenut, zo mima'alotaihem shel g'dolai haru'ach. To be simple is a pedestrian virtue, but to persevere in simplicity is a virtue of spiritual giants.
Sin	751	Lapetach, chatat rovets. Sin crouches at every door.
	752	M'chaseh pesha, m'vakesh ahava. Whoever forgives a sin, he seeks love.
	753	B'rov d'vareem, lo yechdal pasha. When words increase, sin does not cease.
	754	M'chaseh p'sha'av lo yatzlee'ach. Whoever hides his sins will not prosper.
	755	Adam ain tzadeek ba'aretz asher ya'aseh tov v'lo yecheta. There is no righteous person who always does good and never sins.
	756	Choteh echad y'abed tova harbeh. One sinner can destroy a great amount of good.
	757	K'mipnai nachash nus min chet, v'eem tikrav elecha yishcheka. Flee from sin as from a snake; if you go near, it will bite you.
	758	K'cherev peefiyot kol pesha, l'makato ain r'fu'a. Sin is like a double-edged sword; there is no cure for its wound.
	759	Ain adam over avaira ela eem ken nichnas bo ru'ach shtut. Nobody sins unless the spirit of foolishness has entered him.
	760	Ain avera m'chaba torah. A scholar's sin does not cancel out his learning.

A 761   Raishai d'chetya chalai v'sofai mareer.
The beginning of sin is sweet; its end is bitter.

762   Ba'a avaira l'yado v'lo asa ota, mitzva g'dola asa.
If a sin tempts a person, and is rejected, that is
deemed a great virtue.

763   Eem aseeta chaveelot, chaveelot shel avairot, aseh
c'negdan chaveelot, chaveelot shel mitzvot.
If you built up bundles of sins, make bundles of
good deeds to offset the former.

764   Ever shehitcheel ba'avera, mimenu matchelet
hapuranut.
From a limb that started sinning, all the troubles
began.

765   K'feerat ha'avon, shnai avonot.
Denying a sin is a double transgression.

766   Yoter ra mee shegar bain tzadeekeem v'choteh,
mimee shedar bain r'sha'eem v'choteh.
A person who lives among the righteous and
sins is worse than one who lives among the
wicked and sins.

767   Yesh she'he'avon gadol v'hayetzer aino gadol;
li'f'ameem shehayetzer gadol v'ha'avon mu'at.
Sometimes the sin is great and the lusting small;
sometimes the lust is great and the sin is small.

768   Hachet atzmo hu ha'onesh.
Crime (or sin) is its own punishment.

769   Lo ha'avera atzma ma'aveera et ha'adam al da'ato,
ela hata'ava la'avera.
It's not the sin that maddens a person but the desire to do it.

Y 770   An avaira iz shver—nor dos ershte mol.
A sin is difficult the first time.

Slander   771   Kol hamesaper l'shon hara ra'u'ee l'saklo b'even.
Whoever slanders others deserves to be stoned.

772　Eem amarta al achereem davar ra katan, y'hai b'ainecha c'gadol.
If you said a small word of evil about others, regard it as big.

773　Ha'omer l'shon hara hu horeg shlosha: hamesapro, hamekablo u'mee shene'emar alav.
A slanderer kills three: himself, his listener, and the person who was slandered.

774　Kashah l'shon hara mishfichut dameem, migueelul'ee arayot u'me'avoda zara.
Slander is worse than bloodshed, incest or idolatry.

775　Hamecharef bnai adam b'ma she'ain bahem, y'charfuhu b'ma sheyesh bo.
Who slanders others for what they are innocent of will be damned for his own guilt.

Slave (Servant)

776　Eved maskeel chabeb c'nafesh, al timna mimenu chofesh.
Love a wise slave as yourself; do not withhold his freedom.

777　Ha'eved mechomer adono koratz.
A servant is formed from his master's clay.

778　Eved ha'ta'ava yoter m'duca u'm'uneh me'eved bnai adam.
The slave of his own appetites is worse off than the slave of men.

779　Ha'eved m'galeh et teevo ha'ameetee, teva ha'eved, lo bihiyoto eved, kee eem b'he'asoto l'adon.
A slave shows his true character, not while he is enslaved but when he becomes a master.

780　Eved echad aino yachol la'avod shnai adoneem.
One servant cannot serve two masters.

Sleep

781　Al tohav shena pen tivaresh.
Don't love sleep lest you become impoverished.

782   K'ra'eem talbeesh numa.
        Sleep will clothe a man in rags.

783   Shena lar'sha'eem hana'a lahem, v'hana'a la'olam.
        The sleep of the wicked people is a benefit for
        them and a boon to the world.

784   T'cheelat mapala—shena.
        Sleep is the first step toward failure.

Slip of Tongue 785   Kishlon karka tov mikishlon lashon.
        A slip of the foot is better than a slip of the
        tongue

Snake   786   Tov sheba'n'chasheem, r'tzotz et mocho.
        Even with the best of snakes, you'd better
        stomp its head.

Snare   787   Matzeev pach, bo yilached.
        Whoever sets a snare will be ensnared.

Society   788   Al yotzee adam et atzmo min haklal.
        Nobody should withdraw from society.

        A 789   O chavruta, o mituta.
        Death is better than loneliness.

790   Hitchaber el hatzibur she'harai haz'ev yachtof
        min ha'eder hakivsa hato'a l'vad.
        Join the community: the wolf snatches only the
        stray sheep that wanders off from the flock.

791   Kol eleh shebachu v'tzacha'ku yachad shuv ai-
        nam zareem eesh l're'ehu.
        Those who laughed and cried together are no
        longer strangers.

Son   792   Ben chacham y'samach av u'ven k'seel tugat imo.
        A wise son makes his father happy; a foolish
        one grieves his mother.

793   Chosech shivto, soneh b'no.
        Whoever spares the rod, hates his son.

A 794 B'ra cara da'abuha.
    Like father, like son.

795 Ad shnat hashisheet, bincha adon l'cha; ad k'tze
    ha'aseereet eved; ad shesh-esrai yo'etz peleh hu
    l'cha; min hu v'hala ohavcha o son'echa.
    Till age six, your son is your master; until ten,
    he's your servant; until sixteen, a wonderful ad-
    viser; from then on, he's either your friend or
    your enemy.

796 Mutav sheyiv'keh ha'ben me'asher ha'av.
    It's better that the son cries, rather than the fa-
    ther.

Son-in-Law 797 Eem hechatan tov, nosaf l'cha ben, eem ra, ata
    m'abed gam bat.
    If your son-in-law is good, you gained a son. If
    he is bad, you've lost a daughter.

798 Ahavat hechatan lachoten c'shemesh b'yom
    choref.
    A son-in-law's love for his father-in-law is like
    the sun on a winter day.

Soul 799 Eem toveh limshol b'naf'sh'cha, t'na ota
    b'matana l'sichl'cha.
    If you want to control your soul, hand it as a
    gift to your intellect.

800 Yesh lanefesh bree'ut vacholee, c'mo sheyesh
    lagoof bree'ut vacholee.
    Just like your body, your soul can be healthy or
    sick.

801 Bishlom hanefesh yihiyeh shalom l'chol hagoof.
    If the soul is at peace, the body will be too.

Sow 802 Hazor'eem b'dima b'reena yiktzoru.
    They who sow in tears will reap in joy.

Space | 803 | Ha'adam hitzlee'ach l'hitgaber al merchakeem atzumeem v'al hamerchak bain adam l'chavero lo hitzlee'ach l'hitgaber.
Man has succeeded in overcoming tremendous spaces, but not the distance between one man and another.

Spark | 804 | Eeteem adam tzareech l'chatat ba'efer k'dai limtzo nitzotz echad.
Sometimes one must go through the ashes to find one single spark.

Speech | *A* 805 | Chech arev yarbeh ohev.
Gentle speech increases the number of friends.

806 | Lo hamedrash, elah hama'aseh.
Deeds count, not words.

807 | Marbeh dibur y'to'av.
Excessive talk results in scorn.

808 | Kalel omer, u'ma'et harbeh.
Talk little, finish your words quickly.

809 | Hashome'a me'oznecha ma she'ata motzee mipeecha.
Our lips must hear what's coming out of your mouth.

810 | Yesh shnai sugai no'ameem: no'em she'yod'eem merosh kol asher hu ateed lomar, v'no'em she'afeelu l'achar she'siyem d'varav ain yod'eem ma amar.
There are two types of speakers: one we know in advance everything he's going to say, and the other, even after he has finished, no one knows what he said.

811 | K'she'ata pote'ach delet, al tishkach lisgor ota, v'chen ta'aseh l'feecha.
When you open a door, don't forget to close it. Treat your mouth accordingly.

Spring 812 Ha'adama mitchadeshet kol shana; madu'a ain
l'adam aveev kol shana?
The earth renews itself every year. why
shouldn't a person have an annual spring?

Stature 813 Mee sherotzeh l'hagbeeha et komato al y'dai
chaveeshat mitznefet nyar g'voha, o al y'dai
haleecha al kabai etz—aino ela mukyon.
Whoever wants to appear taller by a high paper
hat or walking on stilts is nothing but a clown.

814 K'tzar koma maleh chema.
Men of short stature are often bad-tempered.

Stone 815 Et l'hashleech v'et k'nos avaneem.
There's a time to throw and a time to gather
stones.

Straight 816 To'avat rasha y'shar-derech.
A straight path is an abomination to the
wicked.

817 Aizohee derech y'shara sheyavor lo adam? Kol
shehee tiferet l'oseha v'tiferet lo min ha'adam.
Which is the straight way a man should choose:
The one that honors him and wins people's ad-
miration.

Stranger 818 Torah achat yihiyeh la'ezrach v'laguer hagar
b'toch'chem.
There shall be one law for the citizen and for
the stranger living among you.

Study 819 Yafeh talmud torah im derech eretz.
The study of the Bible together with worldly
pursuits is commended.

820 Arba midot b'yoshvai lifnai chachameem: s'fog,
mashpech, m'shameret, v'nafa.
There are four types of students studying with
the sages: the sponge, the funnel, the strainer,
and the sifter.

821 Al tomar lich'she'ipaneh, eshneh, shema lo ti-
paneh.
Do not say, "I'll study when I'm free"—you may
never be free.

822 Limud mevee leedai ma'aseh.
Study leads to action.

823 Halomed b'simcha b'sha'a achat, yilmad harbeh
yoter mima sheyilmad b'chama sha'ot b'atzvut.
Whoever studies joyously will learn more in one
hour than he who studies longer hours but un-
happily.

Style 824 Adam ne'dar ofee, chasar atzmee'ut, lo yihiyeh
l'olam l'va'al signon.
A man lacking in character and self-esteem will
never be a man of style.

Success 825 Hahatzlacha ha'ameeteet hee hatzlachat
hanefesh.
Real success is success of the soul.

826 Yesh hatzlacha tishak lif'ameem, v'tahadof
b'chema l'achor.
Sometimes success will kiss you, and sometimes
retreat from you angrily.

Sugar *Y* 827 Oib siz biter in hartz'n, vet tzuker in moil nit
help'n.
If your heart is bitter, sugar in the mouth won't
help.

Suspicion 828 Ain adam nechshad b'davar ela im ken asa'o.
No one suspects a person of what he did not
do.

Sweet *A* 829 Lo yada enash ta'ama dimteeka ad d'ta'eem
m'reera.
Man could not have known sweetness until he
tasted bitterness.

830 Al t'hee matok v'timatzetz.
Don't be (too) sweet lest people lick you.

Swindler   831   K'sherama'eem nitkaleem b'adam yashar
b'hechlet, hem merov hafta'a choshveem oto
l'rama'ee gadol mehem.
When swindlers meet a genuinely honest man,
they're so astonished they regard him as a
greater swindler than themselves.

T

Tail 832 V'hevai zanav l'arayot v'al tihiyeh rosh
l'shu'aleem.
It's better you were a lion's tail than a fox's
head.

Take 833 Al tikach b'ones et asher yinaten l'cha b'ratzon.
Don't take by force what will be given you
willingly.

Talent 834 Hakisharon hagadol v'hanadeer
b'yoter—le'ehov kol davar tov.
The greatest and rarest talent is to love
everything good.

Talk 835 Afeelu sichat chuleen shel talmeedai
chachameem tzreecha talmud.
Even the mundane, everyday talk of scholars
needs study.

Tall 836 Gavoha lo yisa eesha g'voha she'ma yetzeh
mehem toren.
A tall man should not marry a tall woman lest
they produce a giant.

Talmud 837 Hatalmud hu ka'yam hagadol.
The talmud is like a vast ocean.

Taste 838 Al ta'am varai'ach ain l'hitva'kai'ach.
There's no accounting for people's different
tastes.

Teacher	839	Mitoch she'ata m'lamed, ata lomed. As you teach, you learn.
	840	Vei latalmeedeem she'rabam rav im eeshto. Woe to the pupil whose teacher quarreled with his wife.
	841	Hakatre'da'ot b 'vatai midrash m'rubeem, v'eelu hamoreem hana'leem mu'ateem. There are many academic chairs but few outstanding teachers.
Tears	842	D'ma"ot potchot sh'areem; zimra mapeela chomot. Tears open gates; song smashes down walls.
	Y 843	Mit treren ken m'nit optzolen choives. You cannot pay your debts with tears.
Thief	844	Hagonev min haganav patur. A thief who steals from a thief goes unpunished.
	845	Lo yavuzu l'ganav kee yignov l'maleh nafsho kee yir'ov. A thief who steals solely to satisfy his hunger pangs is not indicted.
Thought	846	Kee k'mo sha'ar b'nafsho, ken hu. As he thinks in his heart, so he is.
	Y 847	Beser tzu reden mit a froi un denken veguen Gott vee reden tzu Gott un trachten fun a froi. It's better to talk to a woman and think of God than talk to God and think of a woman.
	848	Lachadol lachashov pairusho lachadol lichyot. When you stop thinking, you stop living.
	849	Lakol zman v'et l'chol chefetz tachat hashamayeem. For everything there is a season, and a time for every purpose under the heavens.

850 Et laharog v'et lirpoh.
A time to kill and a time to heal.

851 Et lifrotz v'et livnot.
A time to break down and a time to build.

852 Et livcot v'et lis'chok.
A time to weep and a time to play.

853 Et s'fod v'et r'kod.
A time to mourn and a time to dance.

854 Et lachashot v'et l'daber.
A time to keep silent and a time to speak.

855 Et milchama v'et shalom.
A time for war and a time for peace.

856 Haz'man hu hamelamed hanisgav u'm'chukam
b'yoter.
Time is the wisest and most sublime of teachers.

857 Ma she'ya'aseh haz'man lo ya'aseh hasechel.
What time will accomplish, all your cleverness
cannot do.

858 Ha'zman y'kar ham'tzee'ut; ee efshar liknoto b'dameem.
Time is rare and precious; you can't buy it for
money.

859 Ain davar omed bifnai ha'zman.
Nothing can hold out against time.

Tit for Tat 860 B'mida she'adam moded, mod'deem lo.
As you do, so will be done to you.

Title 861 Vei l'adam she't'arav m'rubeem mechochmato.
Woe to the man whose titles outnumber his
wisdom.

Tolerance	862	Chovato shel hechacham lihiyot ne'eman l'chukai hadat shel artzo v'lo l'vazot chukai hadat shel achereem. A wise man must be faithful to the religious laws of his country, and not scorn the laws of others.
Tongue	863	N'tzor l'shoncha me'ra us'fatecha m 'daber mirma. Guard your tongue from evil, and your lips from speaking deceit.
	864	Marpeh lashon, etz chayeem. A gentle tongue is a tree of life.
	865	Mavet v'chayeem b'yad halashon. Death and life are in the power of a person's tongue.
	866	Kavod v'kalon b'yad halashon. Honor and shame are in the power of the tongue.
	867	Rabeem naflu l'fee naflu charev, v'lo k'nofleem balashon. Many fell by the sword, but more fell by the tongue.
	868	Eem sus ba'al arba raglayeem asu'ee lim'od lif'ameem, mikol she'ken adam she'yesh lo lashon achat. If a horse with four legs can stumble sometimes, how much more so can a man with ony one tongue.
Torah	869	Kol ham'chabed et hatorah, gufo m'chubad al habree'ot; kol ham'chalel et hatorah, gufo m'chulal al habree'ot. Whoever honors the Torah is honored by humanity; whoever dishonors the Torah, will likewise be dishonored.

A 870   Hafach ba, v'hafach ba, d'chola ba.
Turn the Torah this way and that; everything is in it.

871   Chen Torah al lomde'ha.
The Torah sheds its grace on all who study it.

Trade   872   Kol she'aino m'lamed b'no umanut, k 'eelu m'lamdo listut.
Whoever fails to teach his son a trade, it's as though he taught him to rob.

Tradition   873   Hamesoret tzreecha lihiyot keresh k'feetza le'ateed v'lo kursa lish'at m'nucha.
Tradition must be a springboard to the future, not an easy chair for resting.

874   M'soret s'yag latorah.
Traditon is a fence for the Torah.

Translation   875   P'ameem shetzreecheem l'targuem lo et hasheeteen atzman elah ma she'bain hasheeteen.
There are times when one should not translate the lines themselves but rather what is between the lines.

Travel   876   Eesh nosai'a, yodai'a harbeh.
A person who travels knows a great deal.

Tree   877   Kee tatzur el eer yameem rabeem l'hilachem aleha l'tofsa, lo tashcheet et etza.
If you besiege a city for a long time, do not destroy its trees,

878   Kol ha'ilanot l'hana'atan shel habree'ot nivra'u.
Trees were created for mankind's companionship.

879   Ha'etz makeh shoresh rak b'makom echad.
A tree strikes roots only in one place.

Trouble   880   Adam l'amal yulad.
Man was born for trouble.

881   Ain makah ba'olam she'ain la r'fu'ah.
There is no trouble in the world without a cure.

882   Harbeh lamaditee me'rabotei v'yoter misfarei,
u'mitzarotei yoter mikulam.
Much have I learned from my teachers and
books, but most from my troubles.

883   Hatzarot ba'ot maher v'yotz'ot l'at.
Troubles arrive quickly, and depart slowly.

884   Ain l'cha adam she'ain lo tzror.
There's no person without his own bundle of
troubles.

Trust   885   Al tivt'chu bin'deeveem, b'ven adam she'ain lo
t'shu'a.
Don't put your trust in princes, or the sons of
men; there is no salvation in them.

Truth   886   Nikareem divrai emet.
There is no mistaking the truth.

887   Emet tsafa l'mala k'shemen al pnai mayeem.
Truth rises to the top, just like oil on water.

888   Ha'emet k'veda, al ken nos'eha m'ateem.
Truth is a burden, thus its bearers are few.

889   Emet, etz hachayeem—mimenu tochal kol y'mai
chayecha.
Truth is a tree of life—you shall eat from it all
your life.

890   Ain takana l'eleh hayod'eem et ha'emet u'mit-
kavneem limrod ba.
There is no hope for those who know the truth,
but plan to rebel against it.

891   Chatzee emet—sheker shalem.
A half-truth is a whole lie.

892   Mipee katan v'shikor nitan l'galot et ha'emet.
From the mouths of babes and drunkards, you
will learn the truth.

U

Under-standing	893	U'vchol kinyanecha, k'nai veena. With all that you obtain, get understanding.
	894	Knai chochma, knai veena. Obtain wisdom, obtain understanding.
Unity	895	Hineh ma tov u'ma na'eem, shevet acheem gam yachad. See how good it is, and how pleasant, when brothers live in unity.
Unlucky	896	Nofel al hateven v'noguef chotmo b'even. An unlucky man falls on straw, but splits his nose from a hidden stone.
Urgent	897	R'tzoncha she'ye'aseh hadavar miyad, kalech l'cha el hatarud b'yoter. If you want something done immediately, ask the busiest person you know.
Usury	898	V'elu hen hap'suleem: ham'sachek b'kuvya v'hamalveh b'ribeet. These are not qualified to testify or to judge: the dice player, and he who loans money at interest.
	899	Lo dayo aneeyuto, elah she'ata notel mimenu ribeet? It's not enough that the poor man is poor, but you take interest from him, too?

V

Vanity	900	Hevel havaleem, hakol hevel. Vanity of vanities, all is vanity.
	901	L'mad lada'at kee hakol hevel, v'hayu sha'ananeem cha'yecha. Learn to know that all is vain, and your life will be tranquil.
Vengeance	902	Sha'alu l'chacham: Ma hamidot hara'ot? Amar: n'kama. A wise man was asked: What is vice? He replied: vengeance.
	A 903	Omree enashai: D'fara kinhai machareev baitai. One who seeks vengeance will wreck his own home.
Victory	904	Hanitzachon hu gam shikaron m'sucan hamaivee lif'ameem et b'alav lidai atzlut uvatala. Victory is a dangerous intoxication that sometimes leads to sloth and laziness.
Virgin	905	B'tula—vered shelo nift'chu alav. A virgin is like a rose whose petals did not yet unfold.
Virtue	906	Mida tova osa perot Virtue bears its own fruits.

907   Ain mida m'guna shelo tihiyeh to'elet—ma
       bizmaneem m'suyameem, k'shem she'ain mida
       m'shubachat she'ain la nezek bizmaneem rabeem.
       There is no vice that does not occasionally have
       some benefit, and no virtue that at times is hurt-
       ful to some people.

Visit   908   Eem tam'eet l'vaker, tityaker.
                    If you visit less often, you'll be prized more.

Voice   909   Lu b'kol ram yibaneh bayit, kee az banah
                    hachamor shnai bateem b'yom echad.
                    If a house could be built by a loud voice, then
                    a donkay would build two houses in one day.

             910   Kol b'eesha erva.
                    A woman's voice arouses lust in a man.

             911   Kol aveh b'eesha harai zeh mum.
                    In a woman, a harsh voice is a blemish.

Vow   912   Ca'asher tidor neder l'elokeem, al t'acher
                    l'shalmo.
                    When you make a vow to God, don't delay its
                    implementation.

             913   Tov asher lo tidor mi'asher tidor v'lo tishalem.
                    It's better not to vow than to vow and not pay
                    up.

             914   Haneder blee tashlum k'ra'am blee gueshem.
                    An unpaid vow is like thunder without rain.

             915   Hanoder, k'eelu kolar al tzavaro.
                    Whoever makes a vow, it's as though he has a
                    yoke on his neck.

W

War   916   B'milchemet chova hakol yotzeen, afeelu
hechatan mechadro v'hakala mechupata.
In a war of defense, everyone comes out—even
a groom from his room and a bride from her
wedding canopy.

917   Ra'a hee hamilchama, ra'a u'm'usa, aval
ha'anasheem bamilchama yafeem l'itim me'asher
b'chayai yom yom.
War is bad and ugly, but people in the war are
sometimes better than those in daily life.

Warning   918   Ain onsheen elah eem ken mazheereen.
No punishment should be ordered unless there
had first been a warning.

Water   919   Efshar la'olam blee yayeen, v'ee efshar la'olam
blee mayeem.
You can live without wine but you cannot exist
without water.

Way   920   Derech k'tzara hee derech y'shara.
A short way is the straight way.

921   Shlosha d'vareem haderech osah; m'chala hak'sut,
shocha et hagoof u'm'mametet et hamamon.
Travel does three things: destroys your clothing,
bows your body, and reduces your funds.

Wealth

922 K'rov kaspo ya'asheer eesh, v'ach k'rov t'vunato
y'ushar.
The more money, the happier; the more wit,
the happier.

923 Ha'osher yasteer kol mum.
Wealth can cover up any fault.

924 Af al pee she'ha'osher aino ma'ala, hineh hu klee
eleha.
Although wealth is not a virtue, it is an instrument leading to it.

Wicked

925 Ashrai ha'eesh asher lo halach b'atzat r'sha'eem.
Happy is the man who did not walk in the
counsel of the wicked.

926 R'sha'eem omreem harbeh v'afeelu m'at lo oseem.
The wicked promise a great deal but do not do
even a little.

Widow Y 927 Beser a yunguer almoneh vee an alte moid.
Better (to be) a young widow than an old maid.

Wife 928 Eshet chayeel ateret ba'ala.
A good wife is a crown to her husband.

929 Deera na'a v'eesha na'a v'cheleem na'eem
marcheeveem da'to shel adam.
A pleasant home, a pleasant wife and pleasant
furnishings expand a man's mind.

930 Delef tored midyanai eesha.
A wife's bickering is like unceasing dripping of
rain.

931 Kee ba'ada kalon vaboshet, eesha m'chalkelet et
ba'ala.
It's a shame and a disgrace for a wife to support
her husband.

932 Lakol yesh t'mura chutz me'eshet n'ureem.
Every loss can be replaced except the wife of
one's youth.

933   Ha'eesha hee choma l'va'ala.
       A wife is like a defensive wall for her husband.

934   L'ishto shel hashachen yesh tameed yeter chen.
       A neighbor's wife always seems to have more
       charm.

Y 935 Oy va'avoy tzu dem man vos zein froi trogt ze-
       ine hoizen.
       Woe to the husband whose wife wears his trou-
       sers.

Will   936   Eem tirtzu, ain zo agada.
              If you really will it, it will not be a legend.

Wine   937   T'na shechar l'oved v'yayeen l'marai nefesh.
              Give a strong drink to a person who is lost, and
              wine to one in distress.

              938   Kol makom she'yesh yayeen, yesh erva.
              Lust follows on the heels of wine.

              939   Yayeen rubo kasheh lagoof u'm'uto yafeh.
              Much wine is harmful; a little is beneficial.

              940   Yafeh yayeen laz'keneem k'chalav latinokot.
              Wine is good for the elderly like milk is for the
              infants.

              941   Hayayeen y'chadesh ahavat ha'ohev viy'orer et ai-
              vat ha'oyev.
              Wine renews the passion of lovers, and the ha-
              tred of enemies.

Wisdom   942   Chochmot bachutz tarona, bar'chovot titen kila.
              Wisdom cries aloud in the streets; she raises her
              voice in the squares.

              943   Ashrai adam matza chochma.
              Fortunate is the man who has found wisdom.

              944   Tova chochma mip'neeneem.
              Wisdom is more precious than jewels.

945   Ha'adam chacham b'odenu m'vakesh hachochma, v'cha'asher yachashov she'heeguee'a el
tachleeta, hu sachal.
A man searching for wisdom is wise but when
he thinks he has reached his goal, he's a fool.

946   Hachochma hee hayichus hagadol.
Wisdom is a very great pedigree.

947   Chochma blee musar hee k'taba'at blee even.
Wisdom without morality is like a ring without
a gem.

948   Chochma blee mif'al k'etz blee pree.
Wisdom without action is like a tree without
fruit.

949   Chochmat hachochmot shelo y'hai adam
chacham kol ikar.
The greatest wisdom is that a person should not
be over-wise.

950   Chochmat shlomo aina nofelet migourat daveed.
Solomon's wisdom is not inferior to David's
might.

Y 951   Mit chochma alain ken m'nit eienkoifen
shpeizen.
Wisdom by itself does not pay for groceries.

Wise   952   Al t'hee chacham b'ainecha.
Do not be wise in your own eyes.

953   Holech et chachameem yechkam.
Whoever walks with the wise will become wise.

954   Divrai chachameem b'nachat nishma'eem.
The words of the wise are heard softly.

955   Aizehu chacham? Halomed mikol adam.
Who is wise? He who learns from everyone.

956   Al t'hee chacham bidvareem, ach heyai chacham
b'ma'aseh.
Do not be wise in words—be wise in deeds.

Witness	957	Hame'eed edut sheker bachavero rau'ee l'hashleecho baklaveem. One who bears false witness against his friend deserves to be thrown to the dogs.
	A 958	Edut shebatla miktzata batla kula. Evidence that is partially refuted is totally refuted.
Wolf	959	Minhago shel olam: Z'eveem horgueem ha'ezeem. That's how the world is: wolves kill sheep.
Woman	960	Ain derech eesha laishev b'tela. It's not a woman's way to sit idle.
	A 961	Bashta shel eesha m'ruba mishel eesh. A woman's sense of shame is sharper than that of a man.
	962	Eesha m'rachemet yoter min ha'eesh. A woman is more compassionate than a man.
	963	Tov lashevet al pinat gag me'eshet midyaneem u'vait chaver. It's better to live on a roof's corner than with a contentious woman in a mansion.
	964	Ain aiva k'aivat eesha. No hatred is greater than that of a woman.
	965	Asara kabeem seecha yardu la'olam—tisha natlu nasheem. Ten degrees of talkativeness descended on the world—nine went to women and one to everyone else.
	Y 966	A froi zogt a liguen afeelu ven zie iz shtil. A woman lies even when she is silent.
	967	Nasheem am bifnai atzman hen. Women form a separate nation.

968   Eesha, she'aina ela na'a o aina ela chachama,
      harai hee k'mo she'omed al reguel achat.
      A woman who is only pretty or only
      clever—she's like someone standing on one leg.

969   Lanasheem chesron katan—ra itan, u'mar biltan.
      Women have one small defect—it's bad with
      them, and bitter without them.

970   Eesha klai zaina aleha.
      A woman carries her armor with her.

Words   971   Ma nim'r'tzu imrai yosher!
      Honest words are so powerful!

972   Midvarav shel adam ata yodai'a im ohavcha hu
      o son'acha.
      You can tell from a man's words if he's your
      friend or foe.

973   Gam tzipor shilachta od tashuv tz'udena, v'davar
      nimlat mipeecha lo yashuv.
      A bird that you set free may be caught again,
      but a word that escapes your lips will not return.

974   Hamila hee tzila shel hama'aseh.
      The word is the shadow of the deed.

Y 975   Verter darf men opveguen, nit tzelen.
      Words should be weighted, not counted.

World   976   Shlosha me'en olam haba: Shabbat, shemesh,
      v'tashmeesh.
      Three things have a flavor of the world to
      come: Sabbath, the sun, and married love.

977   Hatevel doma l'guesher ra'u'a.
      The world resembles a collapsing bridge.

978   Kol echad v'echad chayav lomar: bishveelee
      nivra ha'olam.
      Every person must say: "The world was created
      for me."

Wound   979   Yeraf'u p'tza'eem v'lo d'vareem ra'eem.
                        Wounds may be cured but not the pain of
                        words.

Y

Years	980	Pirkai Avot roshem et hagueeleem hashoneem shel bnai adam u'ma sheham'soret omeret: Ethics of the Fathers lists the various ages of people and what tradition attributes to each:
Gueel Chamesh	981	Age Five: The age to begin studying Bible.
Gueel Eser	982	Age Ten: The age to begin studying the Mishna (an integral part of the Talmud).
Gueel Shlosh-Esrai	983	Age Thirteen: The age to begin performing religious commandments.
Gueel Shmoneh-Esrai	984	Age Eighteen: The age to get married.
Gueel Esreem	985	Age Twenty: The age to seek a livelihood.
Gueel Shlosheem	986	Age Thirty: The age when one feels one's full strength.
Gueel Arba'eem	987	Age Forty: The age of understanding.
Gueel Chamisheem	988	Age Fifty: The age for wise advice.
Gueel Shisheem	989	Age Sixty.: On the road to old age.

Gueel Shiveem	990	Age Seventy: One's head now turns silver.
Gueel Shmoneem	991	Age Eighty: With luck, one secures special strength.
Gueel Tisheem	992	Age Ninety: One bends beneath the weight of years.
Gueel Me'ah	993	Age One Hundred: It is as though one already left the world.
Youth	Y 994	A yunger man darf leben, an alter man vil leben. A young man has to live, an old man wishes to live.
	Y 995	Men darf nor bet'n oif yoren, keine tsoris vet shoin nit felen. All you have to do is ask for a long life; there will be no shortage of troubles.
	Y 996	Die gantze velt iz a cholem—nor beser a gute cholem aider a shlechte. The whole world is a dream—but a good dream is better than a bad one.
	Y 997	Dos leben iz die greste metzee'a—m'krigt es umzist. Life is the greatest bargain—you get it free.
	Y 998	Az m'lebt, derlebt men. If you live (long enough), you live to see the good things.
	Y 999	Men volt guekent leb'n, nor m'lozt nit. One could really live it up, but they don't let you.
	Y 1000	Yeder mentsh tanz't zich zein tantz, un alle kumen tzu ain tantz. Everyone dances his own dance, and all come to the same dance.

Bibliography

Alcalay, Reuben. *A Basic Encyclopedia of Jewish Proverbs, Quotations and Folk Wisdom.* Jerusalem: Massada Press, 1973.

Babylonian Talmud. London: Soncino Press, 1952.

Baron, Joseph. *A Treasury of Jewish Quotations.* New York: Crown, 1956.

Bernstein, Ignacz. *Judische Sprichvorter* (Yiddish). Wasaw: Fishcher, 1908.

Fischer, Yaacov. *Otzar Pitg'mai Machshevet U'fishraihem* (Hebrew). Jerusalem: 1978.

Holy Scriptures (Masoretic text). Philadelphia: Jewish Publication Society, 1917.

Levanon, Avraham. *Koleerte Perl* (Yiddish). Jerusalem: Rivlin, 1996.

Rosten, Leo. *A Treasury of Jewish Quotations.* New York: McGraw-Hill, 1972.

Rozen, Yechezkiel. *Mivhar Pitgameem Va'amarot* (Hebrew). Tel Aviv: Nitzaneem, 1988.

Shtal, Avraham. *Pitgamai Edot Yisrael* (Hebrew). Tel Aviv: Am Oved, 1978.

BILINGUAL PROVERBS *from Hippocrene . . .*

These anthologies capture the rich language and culture illustrated through the common porverbs of the day. The authors are accomplished writers, academics, and translators who share a common love of language.

The collections are organized:
- Alphabetically by key word
- With their English equivalents
- By English subject in an index

All volumes: 5 ½ x 8 ½ $11.95paperback

DICTIONARY OF 1000 FRENCH PROVERBS
Peter Mertvago
144 pgs   0-7818-0400-0   (146)

DICTIONARY OF 1000 GERMAN PROVERBS
Peter Mertvago
144 pgs   0-7818-0471-X   (540)

DICTIONARY OF 1000 ITALIAN PROVERBS
Peter Mertvago
144 pgs   0-7818-0458-2   (370)

DICTIONARY OF 1000 POLISH PROVERBS
Miroslaw Lipinski
144 pgs   0-7818-0482-5   (568)

DICTIONARY OF 1000 SPANISH PROVERBS
Peter Mertvago
160 pgs   0-78180412-4   (254)

Other Hippocrene Books of Interest . . .

ENGLISH-HEBREW/ HEBREW-ENGLISH
CONVERSATIONAL DICTIONARY, Romanized, Revised Edition
160 pages 5½ x 8½ 7,000 entries 0-7818-0137-0 $8.95pb (257)

ENGLISH-HEBREW/ HEBREW-ENGLISH
DICTIONARY
50,000 entries 604 pages 4¾ x 6½ 0-7818-0431-0 $16.95pb (484)

YIDDISH-ENGLISH/ENGLISH- YIDDISH
PRACTICAL DICTIONARY, Expanded edition
215 pages 4½ x 7 4,000 entries 0-7818-0439-6 $9.95pb (431)

CHOOSING JUDAISM
Lydia Kukoff
152 pages 0-87052-070-9 $7.95pb (181)

THE GLASSMAKERS: An Odyssey of the Jews
Samuel Kurinsky
434 pages 0-87052-901-3 $29.50hc (485)

All prices subject to change. **TO PURCHASE HIPPOCRENE BOOKS** contact your local bookstore, call (718) 454-2366, or write to: HIPPOCRENE BOOKS, 171 Madison Avenue, New York, NY 10016. Please enclose check or money order, adding $5.00 shipping (UPS) for the first book and $.50 for each additional book.